As We
Believe,
So We
Behave

Living The Apostles' Creed

David E. Leininger

CSS Publishing Company, Inc., Lima, Ohio

AS WE BELIEVE, SO WE BEHAVE

Library of Congress Cataloging-in-Publication Data

Leininger, David E., 1944-
  As we believe, so we behave : living the Apostles' Creed / David E. Leininger.
    p. cm.
  Includes bibliographical references.
  ISBN 0-7880-2588-0 (perfect bound : alk. paper)
  1. Apostles' Creed. 2. Christian life. I. Title.

BT993.3.L46 2008
238'.11—dc22

2008018707

For more information about CSS Publishing Company resources, visit our website at
www.csspub.com or email us at csr@csspub.com or call (800) 241-4056.

Cover design by Barbara Spencer
ISBN-13: 978-0-7880-2588-4
ISBN-10: 0-7880-2588-0   PRINTED IN USA

For Christie

Table Of Contents

Introduction

I Believe

It is hard to imagine that one of the genuine heroes of the Bible is never named. He is an unidentified father who has an epileptic son. His boy is sick, subject to violent seizures. Dad has heard the neighborhood scuttlebutt about a certain Nazarene rabbi who had been touring the countryside with a reputation for being able to heal all sorts of diseases. He is not quite sure what to make of the word on the street, but when it comes to your child, you do whatever it takes. He loves his little boy and wants to do something ... anything ... to help him.

This dad is desperate. The medical men of the day had nothing more to offer than just a stick placed between the teeth to prevent injury to the tongue during an attack. The father knows nothing more to do. Then he hears about Jesus. (All three of the synoptic gospels have a version of the story — Matthew 17:14-21; Mark 9:14-29; Luke 9:37-42 — Mark's is the most extensive so we will use that for our study).

This dad has gumption — stick-to-it-iveness. When he and the boy first arrive at the appointed place, Jesus is not there. The teacher and three of his friends are up on a mountaintop retreat. Meanwhile, down in the valley, Jesus' other friends are in the midst of arguing obscure theological details with the local religious establishment when Dad interrupts with a plea for help on behalf of his boy. The disciples give it their best shot, but to no avail — the boy is not healed. No doubt, Dad is now tempted to just give this up as a fool's errand, but something makes him stay put. In a bit, Jesus comes. And that, as we know, makes all the difference.

There is the pre-diagnostic conversation: "How long has he been like this?"

Dad replies, "From childhood. It has often thrown him into fire or water to kill him. But if you can do anything, take pity on us and help us."

Then Jesus answers in a way that sounds a bit sharp and un-feeling at first blush: "If you can!" If you can? If you *can*? There is almost a sense of "How dare you question my ability to handle this!" But that is a misinterpretation. "If you can" must be under-stood in terms of what Jesus says immediately thereafter. "If you can?" Jesus repeats ... then adds, "Everything is possible for him who believes." How true, how true.

The father's response has been repeated over and over ever since: "I do believe; help me overcome my unbelief!" Or in the language of the venerable King James Version that we probably memorized, "Lord, I believe; help thou mine unbelief." What had kept this man there waiting for Jesus, listening to the pious know-it-alls argue over metaphysical mumbo-jumbo? Why did he stay? It is my contention that he stayed because of one word ... *pisteuo* — one Greek word that is translated "I do believe." Not as one who had all the answers, as he himself admitted — "help me over-come my unbelief." He came because of that one word ... *pisteuo* ... "I do believe." He went home happy that night because of one word ... "I do believe."

That one word is at the heart of everything you or I do. What we *believe* determines how we *behave*. We get up in the morning, put our feet over the side of the bed and on to the floor in prepara-tion to stand. Why? Because we *believe* that the law of gravity is as much in force on this new morning as it was last night before we went to sleep. If we did *not* believe that, we would stay right there under the covers. When we leave our home, if we cross the street, we look both ways because we *believe* that iron and steel moving at high speed can make a mess of any flesh and blood with which they come in contact. In the world of work, if we *believe* that regu-larly showing up late for our job (if at all) will get us fired, we come to work on time all the time if we hope to keep working. In interpersonal relationships if we *believe* our spouse is faithful to us, we think no more about it; if we *believe* our spouse is *un*faith-ful, that is *all* we think about. This list is endless. The point is reinforced: What we *believe* will determine how we *behave*!

In fact, what we believe may even determine our level of health. Scientific reports regularly appear indicating that going to church and reading the Bible regularly may do more than save your soul. They may extend your life. In one of the most extensive studies of its kind, Duke University researchers in the '90s found that people 65 or over who faithfully participated in religious activities were 40% less likely to have high blood pressure. In particular, people who attended church weekly and read the Bible or prayed regularly had lower blood pressure than those less interested in religion. It does not take too much searching in a library or on the internet to find studies have shown that religious people are less depressed, have healthier immune systems, and deal better with addictions than the nonreligious.

Even atheists understand. On the best-seller lists in recent years have been titles that debunk religion and belief in God precisely because we behave the way we do because we believe the way we do. Journalist Christopher Hitchens' *God Is Not Great*[1] is an attack on religion as a malignant force in the world, and in light of some of the excesses we have seen — 9/11 being the most egregious example — he does have a point (although, in my view, he goes overboard with it). Oxford Professor Richard Dawkins' *The God Delusion*[2] has gotten some attention. In the preface to the book, he attaches himself to Robert Pirsig's observation that, "When one person suffers from a delusion it is called insanity. When many people suffer from a delusion it is called religion." Sam Harris' angry little book, *Letter to a Christian Nation*[3] begins

> *Thousands of people have written to tell me that I am wrong not to believe in God. The most hostile of these communications have come from Christians. This is ironic, as Christians generally imagine that no faith imparts the virtues of love and forgiveness more effectively than their own. The truth is that many who claim to be transformed by Christ's love are deeply, even murderously, intolerant of criticism. While we may want to ascribe this to human nature, it is clear that such hatred draws considerable support from the Bible. How do I know this? The most disturbed of my correspondents always cite chapter and verse.*

Hmm. "I believe...." What do you believe today? Dr. Donald Miller, the well-known minister and seminary president, tells about a woman who phoned him one Saturday night. "Dr. Miller, what do I believe?" she asked.

"What do you mean?" Miller was not sure he had heard her correctly.

"I mean," she said, "what do I believe? You see, I've just come from a party where several people got into a discussion about their various beliefs. One woman was Jewish, and she told us what she believes as a Jew. Another was Roman Catholic, and she told us what Catholics believe. Somebody was a Christian Scientist, and he talked about what they believe. I was the only Protestant in the group, and frankly, I didn't know what to say. What do I believe?"

"That woman," said Miller, "must have come into the church on *confusion* of faith, not confession of faith."[4] No doubt.

That is not a totally new phenomenon. The obscure little New Testament epistle of Jude comes from (probably) the second generation of the early church when *confusion* of faith began to infect believers. Some teachers had apparently arisen with instruction that did not follow earlier traditions. The accusations of greed and sexual immorality that we find here are often cited in these sorts of polemic texts, but no details are specified. Jude speaks of the opponents as denying "Jesus Christ our only Sovereign and Lord" (v. 4), but that denial was probably a matter of conduct, not confession. Still, there is an insistence that what we believe *matters*. Thus the call to "contend for the faith that was once for all entrusted to the saints" (v. 3).

We are living in a period of history when folks are hard-pressed to articulate their faith. Part of the problem is rooted in our American celebration of "rugged individualism," and its tendency to speak of deeply personal matters only with great reluctance. We have seen public figures make pious pronouncements about their personal faith only to be seen as disappointingly human in their sinful actions — we do not want to be tarred with that brush. But, being painfully honest, the biggest part of the problem is that we have just not done it. It is work, and we have not taken the time nor made the effort to wrestle with the deep truths of our faith. Scripture says, "Always be ready to make your defense to anyone who demands from you an accounting for the hope that is in you" (1 Peter 3:15 NRSV), but most folks could not do it if you threatened them.

If I asked right now, "What do you believe?" could you answer? Yes, you could! In fact, if you are a regular worshiper in a Christian church, you probably have done it over and over and over again. You have probably stood up before heaven and earth and said, "I believe in God the Father, almighty." You said you believed in Jesus Christ, God's only Son. You went on to describe Christ's miraculous birth, his sacrificial death, his resurrection and ascension, and your conviction that he is coming back again. You said you believed in the Holy Spirit and this incredible community of believers called the church. You said you believed in the power of the present and future over the past when you said you believed in the forgiveness of sin. Finally, you said you had a living hope that existence does not end with death, but rather continues with resurrection and life everlasting. And all in barely more than a hundred words. You said *some* of what you believe. That's right, the Apostles' Creed.

By the way, the word "creed" comes from the Vulgate translation of that one word, *pisteuo*, that meant so much to the hero of the gospel story to which we previously referred. The word is *credo*, Latin for "I believe," which just happens to be the way we begin our recitation of the creed: "I believe...."

To be sure, the words, in one form or another, have been around for almost as long as the church. There were local creeds that this congregation or that would use to instruct new converts and those preparing for baptism. (We do not know as much as we might like about them because secrecy was crucial to the church's survival in those early days of persecution.) One with which we have become familiar dates to the middle of the second century and is known as the "Old Roman Symbol." ("Symbol" being the word of choice because all a creed could do, then or now, is offer a "representation" of the faith — no words could ever completely tell the story.)

11

From the Old Roman Symbol developed the statement that has come down to us today.

A word here on the title, "Apostles' Creed." Scholars tell us that it was first identified as such in 390 AD in a letter sent by a church synod to the current pope. Legend had it that it was composed by the twelve after the Ascension with each one contributing a clause. True? Of course not, but the legend was universally believed during Middle Ages. By the time of the Reformation, most scholars had rejected the story while still accepting the creed as genuine apostolic teaching based on scripture. What we recite in the twenty-first century comes from southern France where it probably developed in question-and-answer form in the fifth century.

The Apostles' Creed states the essential facts of the biblical message without elaboration or explanation. Of course, in just more than 100 words, it can only state *some* of what we believe as Christians — it says nothing about justification, sanctification, grace, scripture, social justice, or even love. What it *does* say is powerful beyond imagining.

You say, "I believe in God the Father, almighty." Now what? After all, if what we believe determines how we behave, such a statement will have an impact. What difference should a belief in a personal God who just happens to be creator of the whole universe make in our lives?

You say, "I believe in Jesus Christ, his supernatural birth, his sacrifice, his death, his ascension to glory, and his coming again in power." Now what? What you believe determines how you behave. Is Jesus truly unique? So what?

"I believe in the Holy Ghost." Really? Now what? Speaking in tongues? Dancing in the aisle? What you believe determines how you behave. What does belief in the presence and power of the Holy Spirit mean to our Christian walk?

"I believe in the holy catholic church, the communion of the saints." Is it holy? Is it catholic? Saints? Really? Now what? How do those beliefs impact your behavior?

"I believe in the forgiveness of sins." All sins? Even Hitler's? What does that mean? And if you believe it, do you behave it?

"I believe in the resurrection of the body and the life everlasting." Do you? Okay. So how does that belief make you behave? I *believe*.... Do you? A great preacher of an earlier generation has said, "You don't really believe your creed until you want to say it standing at spiritual attention with the roll of drums in your ears, the light of love dazzling in your eyes, and all the music of a splendid world crashing out a prelude to its truth."[5]

"Lord, I *believe* ... help my unbelief."

1. Christopher Hitchens, *God Is Not Great* (New York: Twelve Books, 2007).

2. Richard Dawkins, *The God Delusion* (Boston: Houghton Mifflin, 2006).

3. Sam Harris, *Letter to a Christian Nation* (New York: Knopf, 2006).

4. John Killinger, *You Are What You Believe: The Apostles' Creed for Today* (Nashville: Abingdon, 1990), p. 11.

5. G. A. Studdert Kennedy, *I Believe: Sermons on the Apostles' Creed* (New York: George Doran & Co., 1920), p. 22.

Questions For Reflection

1. Is there anything we do that does not depend upon what we believe?

2. What other incidents in history besides the terrorist attacks of 9/11 have been religiously motivated?

3. To what extent can we separate motivations when religion may be used as an excuse for particular actions that also has political and economic results?

4. How correct are the critics that religion has caused incredible harm?

5. What are some other affirmations of faith in addition to the Apostles' Creed that you find meaningful?

Chapter 1

God, The Father

"I believe in God, the Father...." Really? Most of us would happily and unashamedly say *absolutely*! Good — that is just what would be expected in a church sanctuary on a Sunday morning or, for that matter, in a mosque on a Friday or a synagogue on a Saturday. In fact, scripture says *big deal*: "You believe that there is one God. Good! Even the demons believe that — and shudder" (James 2:19). In the words of the psalmist, "Fools say in their hearts, 'There is no God' " (Psalm 14:1 NRSV).

Okay — defend your belief. *Prove* that there is a God. You philosophy majors know there are several options (and the rest of us know that this could become really, really boring really, really quickly). Philosophers, if you want to show off, you can spout off the big names for the arguments: There is the "cosmological," the "teleological," the "anthropological," and the "ontological."[1]

Start with the easiest, the cosmological argument. The root word helps us — *cosmos* — the universe. Just look at the whole universe and ask this simple question: "How come?" Birds, bees, rocks, clouds, stars, atmosphere — here they all are. How come? How did they get here? This argument states that this all must be accounted for by some cause equal to the task of bringing it into existence and keeping it going. The cosmological argument insists the answer must be God.

The teleological argument begins with its Greek root meaning "complete" and looks at the universe a little more closely and sees its intricate and amazing design. We look at the structure of a leaf, the growth of a seed, the power of capillary attraction, the stars in their course. Design and purpose seem interrelated in everything about us. Infinite design demands an infinite designer. Does a watch "just happen" without a watchmaker? As has been asked many times: How long would it take 10,000 monkeys hammering on 10,000 typewriters (and monkeys and typewriters would have to be accounted for first) to "just happen" to write the plays of

Shakespeare? The teleological argument insists that this mind behind it all is God.

Of course, one of the most amazing designs in the universe is the human being — *anthropos* in Greek. Thus, the anthropological argument. Humanity involves personhood and has what we call personality; could the human person come from an impersonal source? Humanity is creative in so many ways; was the source of existence *un*creative? Are Bach and Beethoven, da Vinci and Michelangelo, the accidental by-products of an accidental process that began when the primordial slime (wherever that came from) accidentally gathered together to produce the first living cell? The anthropological argument says, "No," the source of this must have been God.

Finally, the ontological argument points to perfection. Several forms of the argument have appeared in the history of thought but that of Descartes is perhaps the clearest. Descartes raises the question as to where this idea of perfection comes from. It cannot be produced from the universe that has in it many imperfections. It cannot come from the person who is demonstrably imperfect; the idea of perfection is actually the person's ideal for himself or herself. Whence this idea, if not from humanity or from the external world, must be from another source; the idea has been implanted by some perfect one. This could only be God.

Four big arguments — if you were not convinced of the existence of God before, do any of those prove it beyond a reasonable doubt for you now? I doubt it. The truth is no argument can *prove* the existence of God. For most folks, there is no need for proof anyway. According to all the surveys in our own nation, year in and year out, 95% of American adults believe in a god of some sort. The name might be different from one person to the next, but there is no need to prove God's existence.

That also happens to be the position of scripture. Nowhere does the Bible ever offer proof about the existence of God. It is just a *given*. We accept it — faith. Go back to the first words of Genesis. At the beginning of the creation story we read, "In the beginning, God...." For the Bible, God always was, always is, and always will be. No argument. That is just the way it is!

So what about this God who *is*? As we say, 95% of us do not doubt God's existence, but we do differ on what kind of God we believe in. You, no doubt, have met some of the contemporary caricatures that attempt to pass for God. Dan Baumann has helpfully identified a half-dozen of them.[2] You may have more:

1. *God as resident policeman.* God is a nagging inner voice. Just about the time you want to enjoy yourself, God blows the whistle. It is as if God were sitting on a cloud somewhere looking down at us and, seeing someone about to have fun, yells, "Now cut that out."

2. *God as parental hangover.* If your parents are kind, so is your God. If, however, your parents are severe and fearsome so is your God. God becomes a whip-carrying disciplinarian who cannot wait for us to do wrong so the punishment can begin.

3. *God as grand old man.* God is pictured as a gray-haired, smiling gent in a rocking chair, a nice old fellow, but not very "with it." God is an archaic remnant of the past, who talks in King James English — lots of *thees* and *thous*. Of course, as with anyone of a previous generation, this God is hopelessly stuck in the past with no concept of contemporary realities.

4. *God-in-a-box.* God must be a member of my group, my social circle, my culture, even my denomination. If I am a Presbyterian, so is God. If I am a Baptist, Methodist, or you name it, so is God. If God were to visit our town, God would, of course, attend our church and no other. God-in-a-box is a provincial deity who is bound by my limited perspective and must think as I do. For example, to consider an issue in the current culture wars, if I hate homosexuals, God must hate them, too.

5. *God as Santa Claus.* God is an eternal disperser of gifts. God's function is to satisfy the selfish requests of earthlings who are perpetually asking. God is viewed primarily as a giver.

17

6. *God as a great computer.* God is a heavenly machine, about as personal as an IBM mainframe. God is mechanical, cold, and impersonal. God set this world in motion, then sat back with no more interest or involvement. God neither knows me nor cares about me.

The list is not exhaustive. Suffice it to say that none of them adequately reflects the God we meet in scripture, and, for that matter, no description would ever be adequate anyway, no matter how orthodox. Remember this: No matter what we say about God, it will never be enough. Read that again: No matter what we say about God, it will never be enough. One more time: No matter what we say about God, it will never be enough. The God of heaven is beyond our human descriptions.

"I believe in God, the Father...." One brief aside here. Some folks have trouble with the phrase, "God the Father." There is the legitimate concern over the gender-specific language. Different traditions explain it in their own way, but, coming from the Presbyterian family, I rely on our recent *Presbyterian Catechism* that says,

> *Only creatures having bodies can be either male or female. But God has no body, since by nature God is Spirit. Holy Scripture reveals God as a living God beyond all sexual distinctions. Scripture uses diverse images for God, female as well as male.*[3]

Why, then, do we keep the archaic language? Simply because it continues to be helpful. It offers us a picture of God's relationship with us (and remember, whatever we say about God, it will never be enough) ... a picture that conveys love and care that is so special between parent and child.

My friend, Carlos Wilton, passes on a story of a five-year-old boy who is trapped in a burning house.[4] The parents have gotten all their children out but this one. There he stands, outlined against a second-story window, surrounded by blinding smoke.

"Jump and I'll catch you," his father cries.

"But, Daddy, I can't see you."

The father shouts back, "I can see *you* — that's all that matters. Jump!" The boy jumps — right into the safety of his father's arms.

"I believe in God, the Father...." Again, we encounter the fact that what we believe determines how we behave. In terms of this affirmation, "I believe in God, the Father...." means we are saying something *more* than I believe that God exists. The key is that little preposition that is so easy to overlook. I believe *in*! — and that *in* is incredibly important.

Here are some examples. I can honestly say I used to believe in my government ... *trust* my government ... to be straight and truthful and to look out only for the good of all. Then came the Pentagon papers, Watergate, weapons of mass destruction, and so on, and I learned I could no longer believe *in* the government. Oh, I could believe that my government existed — all I had to do was check my tax bill, but believe *in* them? No. Or our justice system. I used to believe in that. Then I saw the police with Rodney King and saw that justice depended upon your color, I heard the O. J. Simpson verdict and saw that justice depended upon your bank account, I watched judiciary committee hearings and saw that justice can depend upon your political party. Do I believe *in* the system? Do I *trust* the system? I do not trust anymore.

Do you want to know something I *do* believe *in*? My wife — I trust her completely. I know she will never lie to me, cheat me, steal from me, be unfaithful to me, and will unfailingly have my best interest at heart. If I ask her advice, I know it will be the best she can muster. If I ask her assistance, I know she will offer anything she has. No wonder I love this woman more than my own life! *I believe in her!* And that has an effect on the way I live. I do my best to care for her, support her, and encourage her. I would not be unfaithful to her. I try never to disappoint her. I would absolutely give my life for her. You see, what I believe determines how I behave.

What does it mean to me to say, "I believe in God, the Father?" It means, "Yea, though I walk through the shadow of the next seven days, I will fear nothing ... for my God, this one whom I have come to know in scripture and experience as one who loves me and cares for me even more than my wife does, is with me and has my best interests at heart." That is why I will try to rely upon God's daily presence, to know God's will for my life, and to do my level best to make that will my very own marching orders.

"I believe in God, the Father...." Our closing word is for those of you who, for one reason or another, have terrible trouble saying that, and who wish that you might. How can a person who does not believe in God gain that faith?

Remember that passage in Lewis Carroll's novel, *Through the Looking Glass*, where the Queen tells Alice that she is a 101 years, five months, and one day old. "I can't believe that," says Alice.

"Can't you?" asks the Queen. "Try again, draw a long breath and shut your eyes."

That does not work, does it? Faith in God does not come from shutting your eyes to truth and trying to force yourself to believe what is not so. The answer lies in a willingness to be open.

Start with this. If you believe nothing more than there is a difference between right and wrong, your good sense will tell you that God, if there is one, is on the side of what you believe is right. As you consciously give yourself to the right over the wrong, the God who is there will come to meet you. That is what Jesus meant when his enemies questioned his right to teach, and he said, "Anyone who resolves to do the will of God will know ..." (John 7:17 NRSV). Whenever you are willing to do that much of the will of the highest which you know to be true, you *will* know more. Then the time will come when you too can stand up and, with heart and soul and mind and strength, say, "I believe in God, the Father..."

1. Addison Leitch, *Interpreting Basic Theology* (Great Neck, New York: Channel Press, 1961), pp. 17-19.

2. Dan Baumann, *Dare to Believe* (Glendale, California: Regal Books, 1977), pp. 35-36.

3. Question 11, *Presbyterian Study Catechism*, approved by the 210th General Assembly, PCUSA, 1998.

4. From an unpublished sermon by Carlos Wilton, "By The Light of His Glory," delivered at Point Pleasant Presbyterian Church, Point Pleasant, New Jersey, February 18, 1996.

Questions For Reflection

1. How do you defend your belief in God?

2. Is reference to "God the Father" important to you? Why?

3. How would you react if your pastor repeatedly referred to "God, the Mother"? Why?

4. The author noted some "contemporary caricatures" of God. Did any of them strike a particularly familiar note? Did you think of any not on the list?

5. Of all the technically advanced nations on earth, the United States is the most overtly religious. Why do you think that is the case?

Chapter 2

God ... Almighty

"I believe in God, the Father almighty...." Do you now?

Sometime back there was a short-lived television series called *Studio 60 on the Sunset Strip*. One of the episodes depicted a scene in a hospital where one of the heroes is awaiting word on his fiancée after a particularly dangerous surgery and the birth of their premature daughter. Danny is not particularly religious — in fact, he is not religious at all. But his friend and coworker who is there with him in the waiting room is very religious, and she volunteers either to simply sit with him or to teach him to pray. "Teach me," he says, and she suggests finding the chapel.

They arrive at the chapel and she tells him to get down on his knees. "Why?" he asks. "Respect," she says.

"See, this is my first speed bump," he answers. "I would think that if I were God, I wouldn't have any ego problems. I wouldn't need 'O Lord, creator of the universe, most powerful and merciful and handsome of all the deities,' there's a baby that's two weeks premature, a mom who can't stop bleeding ... If he needs ten minutes of sucking up before he'll fix this, I don't want to work with him."

Danny's friend responds by explaining that getting down on our knees is not for God's benefit — it's for us. We, and especially we who are wealthy and powerful beyond most peoples' imagination, need a level of humility. Danny is still not sure about this whole enterprise and finally asks, "If he's real ..." "He is," she interjects ... "and he loves me ..." "He does," she adds ... "why not just fix it?"

"I don't know," she answers.[1]

Suddenly, we are confronted with the phrase from the creed, "God, the Father almighty..." Right! We hear wondrous claims of a world in the care and keeping of a loving heavenly Father, then look around and see one catastrophe after another. There is Danny's question: "If he's real and he loves me, why not just fix it?"

Lots of people wonder about that. Of all the barriers to belief, none are quite so strong as this one: If this almighty God is so loving, why do so many terrible things happen — hurricanes, earthquakes, terrorist attacks? Is a loving God in control of this world?

The orthodox answer is, "Yes." In the venerable *Westminster Confession of Faith* we read wonderfully Elizabethan affirmation that "God ... alone [is the] fountain of all being, *of* whom, *through* whom, and *to* whom, are all things; and hath most sovereign dominion over them, to do *by* them, *for* them, or *upon* them, whatsoever himself pleases." God is in charge ... of *everything!* The sovereignty of God has always been the bedrock of Reformed theology.

There is an oft-told story of a little boy who offered up this simple prayer: "God bless Mother and Daddy, my brother and sister; and God, do take care of yourself, because if anything happens to *you*, we're all sunk." That is a child's way of acknowledging the sovereignty of God.

In a way, it may seem like whistling through the graveyard to continue with that affirmation. Awful things constantly happen. Some years ago, while we were living in south Georgia, our town was stunned by the crash of a small plane that took the lives of a father, a mother, and their young daughter. I did not know the parents, but I did know Beth. She was a sixth grader, one of my son's classmates. She had performed with our daughter in the local community theater and the two had become good friends. Beth was a gorgeous and vivacious child, one of those who would, as the years progressed, be certain to make many a young man's heart flutter (a process which, I am told, had already begun).

Our daughter was particularly devastated by the news. She sobbed and sobbed as the terrible truth sank in. It made no sense to her that something like this could occur. In the middle of her pain, she began to feel angry. Sunday school theology had taught her that God rules this world, which meant God controls all that happens — even plane crashes. As she sat on my lap, she lashed out through her tears in a way that only an eight-year-old could: "God is not very *polite!*"

24

Later that night, as she lay in her bed and talked with me before saying her prayers, the weeping began again. I tried to explain that even though Beth was no longer here, she was with Jesus — no crying, no pain, a wonderful place. She responded, "God may be happy now, but *I'm not!*" I replied that God was not happy about this. God did not make the plane crash. God does not do things like that. It was a terrible accident, but now God had picked up the pieces and brought Beth and her mommy and daddy home to heaven. My daughter was not mollified — good theology, but cold comfort. She missed her friend.

My son told me that one of the class assignments he and Beth had for English was to keep a journal, and one of the reflections was to deal with those things of which they were afraid. Beth had written that she was afraid of dying young. How ironic!

There are too many ironies in this world for my taste. Bad things happen to good people, and I do not like it. Then how can we continue to preach and teach the sovereignty of a God who loves us more deeply than the most devoted parent with any intellectual or philosophical or even theological integrity?

This is not a new question. In fact, there is even a $3 word attached to it — *theodicy.* It refers to our attempts to show that it is possible to affirm both the "almightiness" of God and the love of God when we are confronted with so much that is awful in the world. There are lots of answers.

Some want to say that what appears to be evil may not be evil at all; for example, an aborigine from the wilds of the Australian bush who is suddenly transported into a modern operating room may see a masked man with a knife about to slice into a helpless patient's flesh and presume this is *terrible* ... but we know it is not. Perhaps you and I are in the same predicament with some of the things we see. Perhaps.

Some want to say that the evil we experience is God's way of keeping us from even greater evil. For example, some years ago, one of the teenage girls in our congregation was killed in a tragic Saturday night automobile accident. Several months later, her mother and I were talking and she opined that perhaps this happened to prevent something even worse from happening to Ashley in the future — a rape or horrible murder or such. I neither agreed nor disagreed, but you get the idea.

Some want to say that suffering is an inevitable piece of the human condition — God cannot be blamed for that. It is human to love, and love is wonderful ... but love can also cause great pain (ask any teenager). Yes, bad things come, but only because we encounter them in pursuit of the good ... okay.

You may have heard the story of the only survivor of a ship-wreck washed up on a small, uninhabited island. He prayed fever-ishly for God to rescue him, and every day he scanned the horizon for help but none seemed forthcoming. Exhausted, he eventually managed to build a little hut out of driftwood to protect him from the elements and to store his few possessions.

Then one day, after scavenging for food, he arrived home to find his little hut in flames, the smoke rolling up to the sky. The worst had happened; everything was lost. He was stung with grief and anger. "God, how could you do this to me?" he cried.

Early the next day, however, he was awakened by the sound of a ship that was approaching the island. It had come to rescue him. "How did you know I was here?" asked the weary man of his rescuers.

"We saw your smoke signal," they replied.

Good lesson — remember it the next time your little hut is burning to the ground — it just may be the smoke signal that summons your deliverance.

As I say, there are many ways people try to understand the existence of evil in a world we say is in the control of God, the Father, almighty, some of which make more sense than others. For what it is worth, folks have been struggling with the issue for thousands of years. The Bible has one whole book that deals with the subject — Job. It is one long poetic compendium of the questions people raise when confronted with catastrophe: Why? Why me? Why him? Why them?

Job's story, of course, you remember. Here was a successful and prosperous man, a man whose life had always been right side up, suddenly confronted with the destruction of his property, even the death of his children as their house collapsed on them. Soon

Job lost his own health — more suffering in a short time than most of us ever endure in our entire lives. He and his neighbors raised those questions. Why? Why you? Why me?

Finally, after Job and his friends had talked enough, the voice of God broke in. "Tell me, Job, where were you when I laid the foundations of the earth? Who hung the stars in the sky and how did he do it, Job? Who tells the dawn to break and the night to fall, and how does it happen, Job? How does the wind work, Job? How many clouds are there, Job?" One unanswerable question after another with our hero finally responding, "Uh, uh, uh ... Gee, Lord, I guess there are lots of answers I don't have." And the Lord says, "*Bingo*, Job! And there are some answers you will *never* have."

One of my contemporary heroes, Dr. Albert Curry Winn, a wonderful pastor and former seminary president explains it as well as anyone.[2] He notes that at the heart of biblical faith we do not find airtight arguments sealed with a "therefore" — all is right with the world, therefore, let us have faith; therefore, let us praise God. Rather at the heart of biblical faith we find things that do not logically follow at all, sealed with a "nevertheless." Much is wrong with the world, the mystery of evil is great, nevertheless let us have faith, nevertheless let us praise God. Perhaps we can better understand the miseries of life if we remember nevertheless.

A little boy in Sunday school prayed fervently, "Dear God, please bless everybody but my brother, Tommy." The teacher replied that God did indeed understand that little brothers are sometimes hard to live with but that God *loved* Tommy. "Then he's a mighty funny kind of a God," the little boy said. In our own way and for our own reasons, we understand.

"I believe in God, the Father almighty...." God is sovereign. God is in control. We continue to preach it, teach it, and confess it. The question remains: Are we just whistling through the graveyard? Are we like little children, trying to affirm what we are afraid is not true by tightly closing our eyes and trying to make our dream real by endlessly repeating our hope? Is this a great collective self-deception? Not at all.

When I need a reminder, I look at the calendar. I see the first day of the week and I remember what happened one Sunday so many years ago ... that first Easter, the day of resurrection. What preceded it had been awful. There was that illegal midnight trial, the taunting and torture. The trek through the city streets under the weight of the wood. The thud, thud, thud of the hammer and the blood that spurted from nail-pierced hands. The agony of the cross being elevated and then dropped with a thump as flesh was torn from the shock. There was even a moment when a casual listener heard Jesus mumble what at first blush sounded like a cry of utter despair: "My God, my God, why have you forsaken me?"

Was it despair? Or was it an affirmation of confidence? You see, the words "My God, my God, why have you forsaken me" are the opening phrases of Psalm 22. The words would have been as well known to Rabbi Jesus as "The Lord is my shepherd" or "For God so loved the world" are to you and me. Just as those passages are so familiar to us, Jesus knew not only the beginning of the psalm but the rest of it as well. Yes, it starts off in the depths of despair ... "My God, my God, why have you forsaken me?" ... but quickly acknowledges, "In you our ancestors trusted; they trusted, and you delivered them. To you they cried, and were saved; in you they trusted, and were not put to shame" (Psalm 22:4-5 NRSV), and then finally soars to:

> *... for dominion belongs to the Lord, and he rules over the nations. To him, indeed, shall all who sleep in the earth bow down; before him shall bow all who go down to the dust, and I shall live for him. Posterity will serve him; future generations will be told about the Lord, and proclaim his deliverance to a people yet unborn, saying that he has done it.* — Psalm 22:28-31 (NRSV)

Yes! This was Friday, but Sunday was coming, and it was that day that guaranteed for time and all eternity that "the wrong shall fail, the right prevail." Remember, as we believe, so we behave. I still cannot adequately explain why bad things happen in a world in the control of a good God, *nevertheless*, I finally let my faith take over and sing Maltbie Babcock's grand old hymn, "This Is My Father's World."

This is my Father's world
Oh, let me ne'er forget
That though the wrong seems oft' so strong
God is the ruler yet.[3]

"I believe in God, the Father, almighty...."

---

1. Aaron Sorkin, "Episode 21: K&R III," *Studio 60 on the Sunset Strip*, NBC, 6/21/07.

2. Albert Curry Winn, *A Christian Primer* (Louisville: Westminster/John Knox Press, 1990), pp. 79-80.

3. "This Is My Father's World," words by Maltbie D. Babcock, 1901.

Questions For Reflection

1. What is theodicy?

2. Have you ever tried to explain a horrible tragedy to someone in terms of faith? How did you do it?

3. If we have difficulty explaining the existence of evil in the world, do we have an equal difficulty in explaining the existence of good?

4. With young Tommy, have you ever felt, "He's a mighty funny kind of God"? In what circumstances?

5. We often hear of the "patience of Job"; in reviewing the Job saga in the book that bears his name, was Job truly patient?

Chapter 3

Maker Of Heaven And Earth

"I believe in God, the Father almighty, maker of heaven and earth...." No surprise. Most churchgoers would have little difficulty acknowledging God as creator of all that is. There may be some disagreement on *how* creation took place — some want to say it happened in six 24-hour days, others want to say the "days" of which we read in the Genesis account should be understood as meaning thousands or even millions of years, still others say it was the "Big Bang." More about that in due course, but, for the most part, we insist that creation did not *just happen* — something ... someone ... was behind it: "God, the Father, almighty, maker of heaven and earth."

This earth and our life on it is truly fascinating. For example, scientists know that the earth's relationship to the sun is not perpendicular — it is tilted at a 23° angle.[1] Is this an accident or is it by design?

While tilted at this 23° angle, our world is rotating on its axis at about 1,000 miles per hour. Scientists say if the rotation was only 100 miles per hour, our days and nights would be ten times as long, and whatever survived the incredibly hot days would freeze in the night when temperatures would plummet to something like 240° below zero.

This 23° tilt is not absolute — it wobbles off by about 3° with amazing regularity. Our seasons and our climates are affected by it. If the world strayed up or down *more* than the 3° tilt, life might perish. Without the tilt to deflect the light and heat, the earth would absorb too much heat. Moisture would be pulled to the north and south poles and build up in tremendous ice caps.

Another thing — the depth of earth's oceans. If they had been much deeper back in the dim and distant beginning, that much more water would have been absorbed or would have dissolved the carbon dioxide and oxygen out of the air. Life could never have begun without an appropriate atmosphere.

Not only are the oceans the right depth, the earth's crust is just the right thickness. If the earth were only ten feet thicker on the outside than it is, that much additional matter would have oxidized all the free oxygen out of the air and life could not have begun.

As we all know, the earth travels around the sun in an elliptical orbit at a fairly constant speed. If our world slowed down, it would be pulled so close to the sun at the shallow or narrow part of that football-like orbit that we would all be burned to a crisp. If we were to slightly more than double our speed, we would be thrown far into space at the long point of the orbit and quickly freeze to death.

Speaking of distance, we are approximately 93 million miles from the sun — just about right to receive neither too much nor too little heat and light to allow us to live. Our moon, while the earth tilts, wobbles, and races around the sun, orbits us at about 240,000 miles, just about perfect for our well-being, controlling the tides and keeping them within livable levels.

Fascinating stuff. Did that all just happen by accident? One would be hard-pressed to defend such a view. On top of all that, what we have is beautiful. Halfway up a mountain road from the port of Charlotte Amalie on the island of Saint Thomas is a clearing that commands a breathtaking view of the sea and the harbor. A sign posted there to indicate the site had been cleared by the hotel at the peak reads: "Lookout Point — Courtesy of Mountaintop Hotel." Below the lettering is scrawled in angry black pencil, "And a little help from God!"[2]

"I believe in God, the Father, almighty, maker of heaven and earth." How did it all happen? Despite what some would have us believe, the Bible does not tell us.

Genesis, chapter 1, is one of two stories back-to-back that describe what happened way back when, "In the beginning...." To be honest, it has caused more than a little difficulty for people of faith in recent years. Some folks have interpreted the material as a scientific treatise giving the details of God's process. Some want to say that the "days" referred to are the garden-variety 24-hour type with which we are all familiar. Others, influenced by scientific studies that indicate this planet is millions of years old, say the "days" of Genesis 1 should be understood as simply distinct periods, each of which may have lasted for thousands of years. Some have argued a "gap" theory that suggests a long period, perhaps millions of years, between Genesis 1:1 and Genesis 1:2, a time when dinosaurs and other unexplained ancient creatures could have come and gone from the earth. Until Darwin came along with his theory of evolution, those were the choices for people of faith.

Darwin struck a nerve. Church folk went apoplectic as they heard this "attack" on the Bible. The most famous of the attempts to hold back the tide of science that was threatening to overwhelm traditional belief was the Scopes' Monkey Trial of 1925. National attention was focused on the little town of Dayton, Tennessee, as young John Scopes, a 24-year-old high school general science teacher and part-time football coach, was charged with violating state law by teaching Darwin's theory. Defending Mr. Scopes was one of the finest legal minds of the day, Clarence Darrow, and joining the prosecution was one of America's premier orators, a three-time Democratic candidate for president of the United States, William Jennings Bryan.

It was a carnival. Banners decorated the streets of Dayton. Lemonade stands were set up. Chimpanzees, said to have been brought to town to testify for the prosecution, performed in a sideshow on Main Street. Opening statements pictured the trial as a titanic struggle between good and evil or truth and ignorance. Bryan claimed, "If evolution wins, Christianity goes." Darrow argued that "Scopes isn't on trial; civilization is on trial."

The prosecution's case began with the court being asked to take judicial notice of the book of Genesis, as it appears in the King James Version. It did. Seven students in Scopes' class were then asked a series of questions about his teachings. They testified that Scopes told them that man and all other mammals had evolved from a one-celled organism. The prosecution rested. It was a simple case, they said.

More witnesses were called, but the highlight of the trial came on the seventh day: according to the *New York Times*, the most amazing court scene in Anglo-Saxon history. The defense asked that William Jennings Bryan be called to the stand as an expert on the Bible. Bryan agreed, stipulating only that he should have a chance to interrogate the defense lawyers. Dismissing the concerns of his prosecution colleagues, he took a seat on the witness stand and began fanning himself.

Darrow began his interrogation of Bryan with a quiet question: "You have given considerable study to the Bible, haven't you, Mr. Bryan?"

Bryan replied, "Yes, I have. I have studied the Bible for about fifty years." Thus began a series of questions designed to undermine a literalist interpretation of scripture. Bryan was asked about a whale swallowing Jonah, Joshua making the sun stand still, Noah and the great flood, the temptation of Adam in the Garden of Eden, and the creation according to Genesis. After initially contending that "everything in the Bible should be accepted as it is given there," Bryan finally conceded that the words of the Bible should not always be taken literally. In response to Darrow's questions as to whether the six days of creation, as described in Genesis, were 24-hour days, Bryan said, "My impression is that they were periods."

Bryan, who began his testimony calmly, stumbled badly under Darrow's persistent prodding. At one point the exasperated Bryan said, "I do not think about things I don't think about."

Darrow asked, "Do you think about the things you *do* think about?"

Bryan responded, to the derisive laughter of spectators, "Well, sometimes."

We know the rest. John Scopes was convicted, given a slap-on-the-wrist $100 fine that was overturned on appeal, not on constitutional grounds, but on a technicality. According to the court, the fine should have been set by the jury, not the judge. Rather than send the case back for further action, however, the court said, "Nothing is to be gained by prolonging the life of this bizarre case."

Yes, there are still folks who say that teaching evolution or the "Big Bang" theory or anything else that does not follow the outline of Genesis, chapter 1, is nothing less than a fiendish attack that comes directly from the devil in hell. I disagree.

Despite what many of us grew up believing, Genesis, chapter 1, was never meant to be understood as a scientific explanation of creation; rather, these verses are a worship tool, adaptable for liturgical use in the congregation, reading antiphonally — first the right, then the left, then all together (see the end of this chapter). The majestic cadence of the wonderful poetry conveys the ultimate truth that "I believe in God, the Father almighty, maker of heaven and earth."

Look carefully at the verses again. Day one: "Let there be light." Where does light come from? The sun. But the sun is not created in this passage until Day four. And the flora and fauna that we know so depend upon the sun arrive on Day three — hmm. No need to press this further. Simply note there is a beautiful poetic parallel:

Day 1: Light   Day 4: Sun/Moon/Stars
Day 2: Waters/Sky   Day 5: Fish/Birds
Day 3: Dry land/Vegetation Day 6: Land animals/People

Was this science? Of course, not. It was faith. It was the ancient theologian's way of saying, "I believe in God the Father, almighty, maker of heaven and earth." How? — Big Bang? — Little Whimper? — we do not know. Let the scientists argue that out.

One brief aside. We noted above that this account is one of *two* creation stories in Genesis. The second one is just as familiar and is hundreds and hundreds of years older — the story of Adam and Eve. It was the ancient Hebrew parent or grandparent's way of answering a child's question, "Where did we come from?" History? Not any more than the account we have been discussing is science. In story form, it is one more way of saying, "I believe in God the Father, almighty, maker of heaven and earth."

What will that affirmation mean in day-to-day life? After all, we continue to insist, as we believe, so we behave. The most obvious response is that if this is God's creation, we ought not to mess it up. The conscious pollution of air and water are prohibited. They do not belong to us. In fact, the opposite is surely true. The Hebrew word that we translate "have dominion" should be understood in terms of care-giving, even nurturing, and not exploitation. We must be careful.

One more thing should not be overlooked. This creator God in whom we say we believe did not just go through those ancient motions to set this old world spinning on its 23° axis and then wander off never to be heard from again. According to the message of scripture, this creator God was busy at the beginning and has been busy ever since.

Remember that the next time you look in a mirror, squint at the reflection, and whisper, "God's not done with me yet." Yes — you know it — God is *still* at work!

"I believe in God, the Father, almighty, maker of heaven and earth" ... and *me!*

---

1. This and the details that follow are from an article by William B. Tolar, Dean of the School of Theology, Southwestern Baptist Seminary, "What Makes Life on Earth Possible?" printed in the Texas Baptist Standard.

2. Irene Corbally Kuhn, "Fun & Laughter," *Reader's Digest,* 1967, p. 557.

The Creation
Genesis 1:1—2:2

Leader: *In the beginning God created the heavens and the earth. Now the earth was formless and empty, darkness was over the surface of the deep, and the Spirit of God was hovering over the waters.*

Right: And God said, "Let there be light," and there was light. God saw that the light was good, and he separated the light from the darkness. God called the light "day," and the darkness he called "night."

All: **And there was evening, and there was morning — the first day.**

Left: And God said, "Let there be an expanse between the waters to separate water from water." So God made the expanse and separated the water under the expanse from the water above it. And it was so. God called the expanse "sky."

All: **And there was evening, and there was morning — the second day.**

Right: And God said, "Let the water under the sky be gathered to one place, and let dry ground appear." And it was so. God called the dry ground "land," and the gathered waters he called "seas."

All: **And God saw that it was good.**

Left: Then God said, "Let the land produce vegetation: seed-bearing plants and trees on the land that bear fruit with seed in it, according to their various kinds." And it was so. The land produced vegetation: plants bearing seed according to their kinds and trees bearing fruit with seed in it according to their kinds.

All: And God saw that it was good. And there was evening, and there was morning — the third day.

Right: And God said, "Let there be lights in the expanse of the sky to separate the day from the night, and let them serve as signs to mark seasons and days and years, and let them be lights in the expanse of the sky to give light on the earth." And it was so. God made two great lights — the greater light to govern the day and the lesser light to govern the night. He also made the stars. God set them in the expanse of the sky to give light on the earth, to govern the day and the night, and to separate light from darkness.

All: And God saw that it was good. And there was evening, and there was morning — the fourth day.

Left: And God said, "Let the water teem with living creatures, and let birds fly above the earth across the expanse of the sky." So God created the great creatures of the sea and every living and moving thing with which the water teems, according to their kinds, and every winged bird according to its kind.

All: And God saw that it was good.

Right: God blessed them and said, "Be fruitful and increase in number and fill the water in the seas, and let the birds increase on the earth."

All: And there was evening, and there was morning — the fifth day.

Left: And God said, "Let the land produce living creatures according to their kinds: livestock, creatures that move along the ground, and wild animals, each according to its kind." And it was so. God made the wild animals according to their kinds, the livestock according to their kinds, and all the creatures that move along the ground according to their kinds.

All: **And God saw that it was good.**

Right: Then God said, "Let us make man in our image, in our likeness, and let them rule over the fish of the sea and the birds of the air, over the livestock, over all the earth, and over all the creatures that move along the ground." So God created man in his own image, in the image of God he created him; male and female he created them. God blessed them and said to them, "Be fruitful and increase in number; fill the earth and subdue it. Rule over the fish of the sea and the birds of the air and over every living creature that moves on the ground."

Left: Then God said, "I give you every seed-bearing plant on the face of the whole earth and every tree that has fruit with seed in it. They will be yours for food. And to all the beasts of the earth and all the birds of the air and all the creatures that move on the ground — everything that has the breath of life in it — I give every green plant for food."

All: **And it was so. God saw all that he had made, and it was very good. And there was evening, and there was morning — the sixth day.**

Leader: *Thus the heavens and the earth were completed in all their vast array. By the seventh day God had finished the work he had been doing; so on the seventh day he rested from all his work.*

All: **And God blessed the seventh day and made it holy, because on it he rested from all the work of creating that he had done.**

Questions For Reflection

1. The author notes that Genesis, chapter 1 should be understood as a worship liturgy, not a science text. How do we tell what kind of literature we are encountering in a particular Bible passage?

2. Is there a contradiction between science and the Bible concerning creation?

3. Controversy over the teaching of evolution has not gone away since the Scopes trial. Should "Intelligent Design" be taught in our science classes?

4. How are we to understand other scientifically difficult scripture passages such as Jonah and the whale or Joshua and the sun standing still?

5. What are some of the priorities that should be held by people of faith in our care for creation?

Chapter 4

Jesus Christ ... Our Lord

"I believe in God, the Father almighty, maker of heaven and earth, and in Jesus Christ his only Son, our Lord, conceived by the Holy Ghost, born of the Virgin Mary...." After all, we call ourselves Christians ... *Christ*-ians. Of course, we believe that Jesus is the Christ.

Be specific. What exactly do you believe about Jesus? Some years ago, in my seminary days, our first course in systematic theology dealt with that question. Our professor described Jesus as "the proleptic, salvific, hidden appearance of the eschatological kingdom of God." Did you get that? "The proleptic, salvific, hidden appearance of the eschatological kingdom of God."

On our way out of class that morning, with the words of the gospel in mind, we chuckled at the whole thing: "Jesus said to the disciples, 'Who do *you* say that I am?' Simon Peter replied, 'You are the proleptic, salvific, hidden appearance of the eschatological kingdom of God.' And Jesus answered him and said, 'What?' "

What, indeed! What about Jesus? When it comes right down to it, we know rather little, at least concerning the details of Jesus' life. Jesus left no record. He kept no diary. He wrote no book. All that we know about him is crowded in a few pages at the opening of the New Testament. You can read it through in a few hours.

The story opens with the birth of a baby in an out-of-the-way town called Bethlehem with his first cradle a manger for the feeding of livestock. He grew up in the unsanitary mountain village of Nazareth with a reputation only for the fact that nothing "good" had ever come from that town. As far as we can tell, it was a normal home; Jesus would have shared normal duties with his brothers and sisters. He knew how to fill lamps and to trim wicks. He knew what housecleaning involved. He knew how to build a fire and could prepare a fish fry. He learned the trade of a carpenter. In other words, a real person, not some figure out of ancient mythology, he was flesh and bone, muscle and blood. He was *real*!

That, by the way, is the point of those phrases, "conceived by the Holy Ghost," and "born of the Virgin Mary." To the early church, the miraculous nature of Jesus' birth was not that big a deal — it is only mentioned twice in the gospels, Jesus never refers to it, the twelve never discuss it, Paul never mentions it. The truly big deal was that he was born at all! This divine character actually took on human flesh, laid aside the "perks" of heavenly office, and became a man.

This affirmation was never meant to prompt or encourage non-Christians into joining the band of believers in response to Jesus' supernatural origins. It was actually to slap down an argument that some Christians had put forward denying that Jesus was the same kind of human being that you and I are. They wanted to say if Jesus was truly divine (as everyone believed), then he was fundamentally different from the rest of us. Rumors even started that he made no footprints when he walked and cast no shadow in the sun. Jesus could not have really died on Calvary, because Jesus is God incarnate, and God cannot die. These are tough issues. But the church insisted from the beginning that this Jesus of Nazareth whom we come to know in the gospels, is not only truly God, but truly human, as well.

As those early Christians repeated the phrase, "conceived by the Holy Ghost," they affirmed Jesus' divinity. As they repeated "born of the Virgin Mary," they affirmed his humanity.

So saying, I cannot move beyond those words without noting the difficulty and even pain they have caused in recent years. Some well-meaning defenders of the faith have chosen the affirmation "born of the Virgin Mary" as a litmus test for orthodoxy. Noting that some teachers and preachers have expressed doubts about the historicity of the virgin birth, "true believers" have gone ballistic and started incredible and bitter ecclesiastical wars in an attempt to defend the veracity of scripture and the deity of Christ.

Well, as we noted in our consideration of Genesis, chapter 1, "truth" may be one thing to one person and something entirely different to another — to one it may be that God created light on the first day and the sun on the fourth day — to another it may simply be that God created. In the current discussion, the word we translate as "virgin" from scripture can just as easily be translated "young woman," so to make a dogmatic case one way or the other is impossible.

To defend Christ's deity, there are better ways than by using this phrase. The creed itself affirms it in calling Jesus God's "only Son." True, we believe in "God, the Father ..." and that, in a special way, we are all God's children. But we also insist that Jesus is unique. Listen to the writer of the epistle to the Hebrews:

> *Long ago God spoke to our ancestors in many and various ways by the prophets, but in these last days he has spoken to us by a Son, whom he appointed heir of all things, through whom he also created the worlds. He is the reflection of God's glory and the exact imprint of God's very being, and he sustains all things by his powerful word.*   — Hebrews 1:1-3a (NRSV)

That is no description of you or me. If Jesus is God's *only* Son, does that put the rest of us down? No — exactly the opposite, in fact. The very idea that Jesus would take on flesh and blood and become one of us is incredible, and elevates us beyond measure. "I believe in ... Jesus Christ, [God's] only Son, our Lord, conceived by the Holy Ghost, born of the Virgin Mary...."

One last aside on this virgin birth question — for myself, I prefer to believe the traditional understanding about Jesus' miraculous birth — "conceived by the Holy Ghost, born of the *Virgin* Mary" — that feels more comfortable than an admission that Jesus was born out of wedlock to folks who could not control themselves. To those who cannot believe as I do, take heart ... I do not consign you to unending hell.

Back to Jesus — we believe he was a real person, both human and divine, God's *only* Son. We also believe he was Jesus *Christ*. At about thirty years of age, Jesus laid aside the tools of his trade and began to teach, preach, and heal. From the beginning, people reacted to him. Little children ran at the sound of his voice, the aged found comfort in his presence, the sick found healing by merely touching the hem of his garment. He had his hours of popularity when the multitudes gathered 'round. He had his moments of quiet reflection, either alone, or with those closest to him. It was on just such an occasion that we encounter the dialogue between Jesus and the twelve, "Who do you say that I am?" Simon answers, "You are the Messiah (from the Hebrew), [or] the Christ (the Greek equivalent of Messiah), the Son of the living God" (Matthew 16:16 NRSV).

Christ is not Jesus' surname. It is a title. It indicates "the anointed one" — someone set apart for God's service. This was God's representative. In the Old Testament the title was regularly applied to the king. By the time of Jesus, the Jewish people were looking for a Messiah, a Christ, to come who would lead them in victory against their oppressors, a conquering hero who would overthrow the hated Romans. As soon became evident, this was not God's intention in Jesus. For those who had their hopes pinned on a military Messiah, this was a devastating blow. Indeed, some have speculated that this was Judas' problem — once he found out that his dream of conquest was over, he bolted ranks. And the rest of the story we know too well.

Jesus was betrayed by those he trusted, abandoned by those he loved. A purple robe was thrown contemptuously across his shoulders, a crown of thorns jammed down upon his brow. He carried his own cross, as far as he was able, to an outlaw's execution. The life that had begun in humble obscurity ended in public shame. He who, at birth, had been laid in a borrowed manger was now laid away in a borrowed tomb.

We know the story does not end there. And that is why we can continue to affirm, "I believe in Jesus Christ ... our Lord!"

Lord — what does the name mean? To the ancients, it meant master or owner and was always a title of consummate respect. In the modern world, to call Jesus "Lord" is to say he is the chief, the boss, the main man, the head honcho. The buck stops with him; his decisions are final. Hear the "Declaration of Faith" written by the Southern Presbyterians a few years ago:

> We declare that Jesus is Lord.
> His resurrection is a decisive victory
>   over the powers that deform and destroy human
>   life.

His Lordship is hidden.
The world appears to be dominated by people and
systems that do not acknowledge His rule.
But His Lordship is real.
It demands our loyalty and sets us free
from the fear of all lesser lords who threaten us.
We maintain that ultimate sovereignty now belongs to
Jesus Christ in every sphere of life.
Jesus is Lord!
He has been Lord from the beginning.
He will be Lord at the end.
Even now He is Lord.[1]

Jesus Christ is Lord! These four words were the first creed that the Christian church ever had. To be a Christian then and to be a Christian now is to make that affirmation. If someone can say, "For me, Jesus Christ is Lord," that person is a Christian.

All along we have been insisting that as we believe, so we behave:

- If we say that "Jesus Christ is Lord," it means that, for us, Jesus Christ is uniquely in charge — we are prepared to obediently follow in whatever direction the Lord chooses to lead, even if he goes where we might rather he did not.
- If we say, "Jesus Christ is Lord," that means his priorities will become our priorities. We will be drawn to those on the margins, the outcasts, and even those society (and sometimes even the church) suggests we stay away from.
- If we say, "Jesus Christ is Lord," we will take religion seriously — we will worship, we will fellowship, we will pray, we will even sacrifice ... just as Jesus did, and we will never let religion become an end in itself; it must never get in the way of people.
- If we say, "Jesus Christ is Lord," it means we are prepared to give to Jesus a love and a loyalty that will be given to no other person in all the universe.

45

"Jesus Christ is Lord." It may be that you cannot put into words who and what you believe Jesus to be, but so long as there is in your heart this wondering love, and in your life this willingness to obey, you are a Christian.

Millions upon millions of words have been written and spoken about Jesus. As Emerson once noted, "The name of Jesus is not so much written as *ploughed* into the history of the world." But none of that history has ever been able to tell the whole story. As that great preacher of the nineteenth century, Horace Bushnell, once said, "Who can satisfy himself with anything he can say concerning Jesus Christ?"

Malcolm Muggeridge, for most of his life a skeptic, following his conversion became wonderfully reflective. In his book, *Jesus Rediscovered*, writes,

> *Beneath the Church of the Nativity in Bethlehem, a silver star marks the alleged precise spot where Christ was born. A stone slab nearby is supposed to mark the exact site of the manger wherein he lay. The Holy Land is littered with such shrines, divided up like African territories in the old colonialist days, between the different sects and denominations — the Greeks, the Armenians, the Copts, the Latins, etc. — and often a cause of rancor among them. Most of the shrines are doubtless fraudulent, some in dubious taste, and none to my liking. Yet one may note, as the visitors come and go, ranging from the devout to the inanely curious, that almost every face somehow lights up a little.*[2]

There is something about Jesus. And the question to the disciples comes again: "Who do *you* say that I am?" You must answer. I would not expect your response to say anything about "proleptic" or "salvific" or "eschatological." Rather, with Simon Peter, say with every fiber of your being, "You are the Christ, the Son of the living God."

"I believe in God, the Father, almighty, maker of heaven and earth and in Jesus Christ, His only Son, our Lord...."

1. The 197th General Assembly (PCUSA, 1985) made its own the action of the 177th General Assembly (PCUS, 1977) with reference to A Declaration of Faith which is as follows: "That 'A Declaration of Faith' be adopted as a contemporary statement of faith, a reliable aid for Christian study, liturgy, and inspiration ..." (*Minutes*, PCUS, 1977, Part I, p. 168).

2. James S. Hewett, *Illustrations Unlimited* (Wheaton, Illinois: Tyndale House Publishers, Inc., 1988), p. 74.

Questions For Reflection

1. What does the affirmation "Jesus Christ is Lord" mean to you?

2. Use some creative imagination — what do you think Jesus' childhood was like?

3. Did Jesus have a sense of humor? Give some examples.

4. According to what we read in the gospels, what can we identify as Jesus' priorities?

5. What convinces you that Jesus is divine as well as human?

Chapter 5

Suffered ... Dead ... Buried

"I believe in God, the Father almighty, maker of heaven and earth, and in Jesus Christ his only Son our Lord, who was conceived by the Holy Ghost, born of the Virgin Mary, suffered under Pontius Pilate, was crucified, dead, and buried...."

They killed him. They taunted him ... tortured him. They killed him. Why? What had he done? The answer of our faith over the centuries has been *nothing*. He was the only perfect one who ever lived. He was sinless. Yet, the record remains and our affirmation is repeated: "... suffered under Pontius Pilate, was crucified, dead, and buried...." Why?

The traditional answer, of course, is that "Christ died for our sins" (1 Corinthians 15:3). The Bible says so. Our youngest Sunday school students know it. John the Baptist declared, "Look, the lamb of God who takes away the sin of the world" (John 1:29). His horrible death paid the penalty that would have been exacted of you and me without this selfless sacrificial act of redemption on Calvary:

> *Jesus paid it all,*
> *All to him I owe;*
> *Sin had left a crimson stain,*
> *He washed it white as snow.*[1]

Have you ever wondered about that? I would not be surprised if you answered, "No." After all, this is pretty bloodthirsty stuff. If it were not for the fact that it has been part and parcel of our faith tradition from the time we were old enough to understand anything, we would be horrified. If this story was not so familiar to us, if we were hearing it for the first time from someone trying to convert us to his or her faith, we would gag. We are talking about *human sacrifice* here. In how many other situations would we blithely accept human sacrifice as a good thing? In any other religion? What are we saying about the God we worship with this human sacrifice business? I thought we also learned early on in Sunday school that our God is *love*! Are these contradictions or questions?

If it eases your mind, digging into this is nothing new. For centuries, theologians have wondered about this question of why Christ died and how that death has anything to do with our salvation. The $3 theological word for the subject is atonement. There have been a number of attempts at explaining it.

There is the "moral-influence" theory that emphasizes the effect Christ's sufferings have (or should have) on us. We see what misery he went through on our behalf and we respond in a positive way.

An incident in the life of Gandhi can illustrate. In 1922, the independence movement in India was beginning to pick up tremendous momentum and along with it, a deep-seated hatred for the British. Gandhi, of course, was a leading light in that movement and a strong believer in its eventual success but only if the struggle were carried on by nonviolent means. When word came to him that some of his own followers in the movement were beginning to disregard this principle of non-violence, he announced that he would not eat until *all* their violence was at an end and that they would guarantee that violent acts would not recur. As the days passed, it became obvious that Gandhi was in dead earnest and was willing to *die* unless the violence stopped and assurances were forthcoming that such acts would not be repeated. So the violence stopped. Gandhi was weakened to the point where the doctors could not be sure that he would live even if the fast were ended. Then the guarantees were given; the fast was broken and Gandhi recovered. Through his suffering, he had so affected even those who disagreed with him that they were willing to give up what their leader considered wrong methods. Such is the stuff of moral influence.

This is what some scholars want to say concerning the way the death of Christ affects us. We see what he went through and are so moved that we renounce our evil and everyone lives happily ever after. The only problem is there are lots of folks who have never heard the story, so they cannot respond.

Another approach, the "ransom to the devil" theory. This one has the devil offering God the souls of all humanity in exchange for the one sinless soul, Jesus Christ. The theory went on to say that this is precisely what happened, but God hoodwinked the devil by raising Jesus up after only three days. Christ was simply the bait on a clever, divine fishhook that was snatched away at the opportune moment. Is God that kind of a charlatan?

Another theory is "penal substitution." This is the one with which most of us best identify as far as our early training goes. It takes a legal approach and says that if God's laws are broken, a penalty must be paid (the same way as in our own legal system). This theory says that what Jesus did was to live a life of perfect obedience to God's law and needed no penalty payment for himself. Thus, he and he alone was able to pay the penalty on our behalf to satisfy the demands of a righteous, heavenly judge. Justice is served. Of course, there is a basic flaw in the argument. Simply because an injured party has restitution paid on behalf of the one who caused the injury in the first place in no way restores the original relationship. There is no reconciliation there, not in any meaningful sense.

There is one more theory — the "satisfaction" theory. This is similar to the one we just discussed. It recognizes the substitutionary character of Christ's death — he did it on our behalf; it recognizes the human offense against God, but insists that the offense is not just against God's law but against God's *honor*. The way the theologians described it, the price of satisfaction was higher than you or I could pay, so God had two choices: Be content with the fact that there is a gap that could not be bridged, or *find* some way to bridge the gap. According to this theory, God took the second option. God became a human being so no one could say that the satisfaction was not legitimate, and then God paid the price ... a price paid *by* God *to* God. That is why God became human and that is how any atonement has taken place.

Let us try one more. Perhaps, way back when Paul wrote "Christ died for our sins," everyone knew exactly what he meant, more so than we might today. Perhaps there was some perspective, shared by those of that time and in that society, which understood the relationship between Christ's death and our sinfulness. Perhaps if we could read those words through their eyes, it would all make a bit more sense. Remember that the concept of family in the Middle East is incredibly important, far more so than here in the West. Oriental cultures think nothing at all of four generations living under the same roof — they do not raise their children to leave. Tied in with that is a special understanding of what it means to be family, not only in terms of mutual support, but also of family honor and family shame. A person may be guilty, but that guilt has a ripple effect — the person's family members and tribe will end up feeling shame.

We understand that to a degree. What are the feelings of the parents and siblings of someone on trial for murder or rape or something equally horrible — shame? — probably. Did they commit the crimes? No, but the shame is there, nonetheless. By the same token, an individual may be recognized for some accomplishment or great deed. Not only is that individual honored, the honor also rubs off on the entire family. When one of our own does something honorable and is honored for it, we are honored. We experience family shame and honor feelings here in the West even though we, more than any of the other cultures on earth, insist on putting individuals on a pedestal. So saying, note that those feelings are intensified in parts of the world that place a high value on interrelatedness, extended family, and tribe.

In ancient Mediterranean society, shame was often cancelled through blood — still is. If one shames me or my kin, I may restore honor by killing the offender. Or I may attempt to reduce my shame or that of a loved one by spilling my own blood (as Saul did after his failures as king, or as Judas did after betraying Jesus). Even today, in Palestinian culture, a father may be honored for killing his own unmarried daughter if she shames her family by becoming pregnant.

Move the family metaphor up to the nth degree — the human family. In Paul's writings, he notes our human interrelatedness, especially in terms of sin — he harks back to Adam, the sin that began in the Eden, the sin that has infected us and shamed the human family ever since (Romans 5:12-19; 1 Corinthians 15:22 ff). Along came Jesus. He took on our family shame. He was killed by the most shameful means possible, the public humiliation of crucifixion. The Jews regarded death on a cross as evidence of rejection by God: "Anyone hung on a tree is under God's curse," says Deuteronomy 21:23. Jesus died in utter shame. In a society that understood the way shame could be washed away by blood, Jesus "... suffered under Pontius Pilate, was crucified, dead, and buried...." "... and the blood of Jesus ... cleanses us from all sin" (1 John 1:7 NRSV).

We believe it. Now what difference does it make in your life? If what we believe determines how we behave, what are the implications?

One of my seminary professors, years ago, told the story of three young university students in Paris. As is the case with many who get to their late teens and early twenties without too much terrible happening to them, they looked at the world with jaundiced eyes. All the values they had been taught by their parents were terribly foolish and outmoded. The religion they had been taught as children was nothing more than infantile superstition. Their creed had become "Science is my shepherd, I shall not want."

One day, as they walked in the city, they happened to pass by the cathedral of Notre Dame. They looked at that magnificent structure and laughed among themselves at the foolishness of the peasants centuries before who had worked so hard and given up so much to honor something as absurd as the Christian faith. One said to the others, "I am tempted to go in there right now and tell the priest what a misguided imbecile he is and how little his Christ is worth."

The other two said, "Go ahead. We dare you." And so, not one to let the challenge go unheeded, he went, his friends following at a little distance.

Into that magnificent building he came, straight down to the main altar where he saw a priest busy with some work. There was no mass going on, so the young man went right up to him and said, "Father, Christ died for my sins, and I don't give a damn."

Needless to say, the man of the cloth was taken aback. What does one say?

"Didn't you hear me, Father? I said Christ died for my sins, and I don't give a damn."

"Oh, I heard you, my son, but I'm not the one you should be telling." Then the priest pointed up above his head to the lifelike crucifix over the altar and said, "You really should say it to him."

A sneer crossed the boy's lips as he said, "Sure!" Then he looked up and saw the figure of another young man, not much different from himself: strong, lean, in the prime of life, but sad somehow, as if the weight of the whole world had been put on him. As the boy continued to look, he said again, "Christ died for my sins ... and I don't give a damn." Then he looked away from the crucifix and back to the priest. "There, I've said it to him."

But the good father was not satisfied. He said, "Please, my son, do it again ... please."

Again, the boy agreed. His eyes returned to that lifeless figure above him: young and strong in body, but with flesh ripped apart by nails in the hands, the wound of a spear in the side, the crown of thorns jammed down on the brow. It was the picture of suffering the lad had never noticed before. He opened his mouth to speak once again: "Christ died for my sins, and ... and...." But he could not finish. He fell to his knees and began to sob.

It is the closing scene in the motion picture, *Ben Hur*. The sky is disappearing behind the ominous-looking cloud formations. The movie camera takes a long shot of three crosses rising out of a distant hill. Then the camera moves in close, closer, to the figure stretched out on the center cross. Lightning reveals a man squirming in silent agony to the rhythm of the flashes. It is raining hard. With each flash of light, the pool of rainwater at the foot of the cross grows larger. Suddenly, a single drop of blood drips into the pool and scatters. Then another drop falls. And then another. The pool is now tinted light red. The rain comes harder and the pool overflows into another pool immediately below it. The second pool reddens and enlarges, overflowing into still another pool which, in turn, overflows into a small stream. The bloodstained stream flows into a larger stream that meets a river that flows into an ocean.

"... crucified, dead and buried." Why? For me — for you — for all the world ... "that whoever believes in him shall not perish but have eternal life" (John 3:16).

_____

1. "Jesus Paid It All," words by Elvina Hall, 1865.

Questions For Reflection

1. What is atonement?

2. Of the atonement theories noted by the author, which most resembles the teaching of your church tradition?

3. If the concept of human sacrifice is so abhorrent to Christians, how do we understand the crucifixion?

4. If the cross is an instrument of torture and an early method of capital punishment, how do we justify turning crosses into jewelry?

5. Is it difficult to read the Bible through first-century Middle Eastern eyes for Christians raised 2,000 years later in the West?

Chapter 6

He Descended Into Hell

"I believe in God, the Father almighty, maker of heaven and earth, and in Jesus Christ his only Son our Lord, who was conceived by the Holy Ghost, born of the Virgin Mary, suffered under Pontius Pilate, was crucified, dead, and buried. He descended into hell."

Hell — it's a fascinating subject to many people. According to an ABC News *20/20* program, it is far more fascinating than heaven — they devoted an entire prime-time hour to the subject.[1] The program noted that the "Encyclopedia of Hell" (I didn't even know there was such a thing) outsells the "Encyclopedia of Heaven" (I didn't know there was one of those either) by ten to one.

Perhaps we should not be surprised. One of the classics of medieval literature is Dante's *Divine Comedy*, which begins with the poet passing through the gate of hell, on which is inscribed the famous phrase, "Abandon all hope, ye who enter here." Dante meets the Roman poet, Virgil, who plays tour guide through the nine circles of hell. The circles are concentric, each new one representing worse and worse expressions of evil, culminating in the center of the earth, where Satan is held, bound. Each circle's sin is punished in a fashion fitting the crime: Traitors are encased in ice symbolic of the coldness of their treachery; gluttons must lie in the filth of a pig sty; hypocrites go about in heavy, lead cloaks that are covered with a thin layer of gold. My favorite — flatterers are steeped in human excrement. Punishment to fit the crime.

In the seventeenth century, John Milton's *Paradise Lost* opens with the fallen angels, including their leader, Satan, waking up in hell after having been defeated in the war in heaven. Milton portrays hell as the abode of the demons and the passive prison from which they plot their revenge upon heaven through the corruption of the human race.

In the eighteenth century, "Sinners in the Hands of an Angry God" became one of the most famous sermons ever preached.

Jonathan Edwards, a prominent Calvinist Congregational minister, delivered it first in his home parish of Northampton, Massachusetts, where it met with little reaction. It was his second presentation in Enfield, Massachusetts (now Enfield, Connecticut), in 1741 that prompted the famous accounts of widespread weeping, fainting, crying out, and convulsions from members of the congregation.

> The pit is prepared, the fire is made ready, the furnace is now hot, ready to receive them; the flames do now rage and glow. The glittering sword is whet, and held over them, and the pit hath opened its mouth under them. The devil stands ready to fall upon them, and seize them as his own....[2]

Glory!

Now, in the twenty-first century, some still hold on to the "lake of fire" image that comes from the book of Revelation (20:14-15). Others are worried that a literal understanding does violence to our understanding of the God of love whom we come to know in Jesus Christ and who wants nothing more than the salvation of all humanity (1 Timothy 2:4).

Several years ago, I decided I wanted to learn Spanish and I have been working at it ever since. One of my efforts involves a daily Spanish word from the internet that is then explained further by use in a sentence.[3] Not long ago, the word of the day was *dulcificar*, which means to sweeten, to make more palatable, to make milder or more mellow, to make less harsh. The example used was this: *"Ahora las religiones se dulcifican. En nuestros días, ¿quién cree en el infierno?"* Translated, that means, "Religions are more mellow now. In our day, who believes in hell?" That *20/20* program mentioned earlier in this chapter noted that a decade ago, 56% of Americans polled by Gallup and Harris said they believed in hell; after the terror attacks of September 11, 2001, the number shot up to 71%.

Somewhere, I read of a college drama group that presented a play in which one character would stand on a trapdoor and announce, "I descend into hell!" A stagehand below would then pull a rope, the trapdoor would open, and the character would plunge through. The play was well received.

When the actor playing the part became ill, another actor who was quite overweight took his place. When the new actor announced, "I descend into hell!" the stagehand pulled the rope, and the actor began his plunge but became hopelessly stuck. No amount of tugging on the rope could make him descend.

One student in the balcony jumped up and yelled: "Hallelujah! Hell is full!"

Back to our subject at hand: "He descended into hell." Some housekeeping details about these four words. First, every congregation does not repeat them. In fact, seminarians are often facetiously (or not) advised to ask, when going out on preaching assignments to unfamiliar congregations, "Does this church go to hell?" In my Presbyterian tradition, the old red hymnal from the 1950s that many of us used until the current blue hymnal came out sets the phrase apart in brackets with an asterisk noting, "Some churches omit this." (The hymnal we use now makes no such note; I will discuss this later.)

One of my pastorates was with a congregation in North Carolina that did not say these words. One of the charter members explained that in the early days of that church, there was a variety of denominational backgrounds that had come together. Some had little or no experience with reciting creeds in worship, some had reservations about certain affirmations in *this* creed (in particular, "He descended into hell"), and one concerning belief in the "holy catholic church." After a rousing discussion, a compromise was reached: no "descended into hell," but they kept the "holy catholic church" since the affirmation only referred to the universality of the church and not any tie to the Catholic church of Rome.

All in favor say, "Aye" — opposed, "Nay." The ayes have it. The motion is agreed to. And *that*, good friends, is precisely the way difficult doctrinal issues have been settled in the church for centuries. If you had the votes, you were a winner; if you did not, not only did you lose, you were a heretic — literally.

This is probably the way the affirmation made it into the creed in the first place. The words were *not* in the earliest versions of the creed. In fact, we do not run into them at all until about 400 years after Christ. The other ancient statement of faith, the Nicene Creed, makes no mention of any descent into hell. Why not? Perhaps two reasons: one, "hell" is really a mistranslation of the original statement that only affirmed that Christ descended to the *dead* — the early church made a distinction between the place where dead folks went before judgment ... *hades* in Greek, *sheol* in Hebrew ... and this place of eternal punishment; and two, because a statement such as this could be seen as simply a redundancy since we already have a word saying he was "crucified, dead, and buried." Either way, at some point, some theologian in some church council, somewhere, called for a vote, and the result is what we have now.

If you wonder why, the answer goes back to scripture. In 1 Peter we find,

> *For Christ died for sins once for all, the righteous for the unrighteous, to bring you to God. He was put to death in the body but made alive by the Spirit, through whom also he went and preached to the spirits in prison who disobeyed long ago....*   — 1 Peter 3:18-20

What those who want to use this as biblical warrant for "He descended into hell" in the creed would have us believe is that between the time of Christ's death on the cross and resurrection from the tomb, he was busy. He went to this place of the dead ... *hades, sheol* ... proclaimed the gospel and led these "prisoners" to paradise. A third-century Syrian creed speaks of Jesus, "who was crucified under Pontius Pilate and departed in peace, in order to preach to Abraham, Isaac, and Jacob and all the saints concerning the end of the world and the resurrection of the dead."

There are any number of artistic representations of the story. One of the more famous is a painting by Baldovinetti that hangs in the Museum of San Marcos in Florence showing Christ standing on the gate of hell that has been knocked off its hinges. Under the gate lies the struggling devil as crowds of people happily escape. In the Middle Ages, this became known as the *Harrowing of Hell*.

Is that what happened — really? To be painfully honest, we have no idea. So saying, listen to the wisdom of William Barclay:

> *Many in repeating the creed have found the phrase "He descended into Hell" either meaningless or bewildering, and have tacitly agreed to set it on one side and forget it. It may well be that we ought to think of this as a picture painted in terms of poetry rather than a doctrine stated in terms of theology. But it contains these three great truths — that Jesus Christ not only tasted death but drained the cup of death, that the triumph of Christ is universal, and that there is no corner of the universe into which the grace of God has not reached.*[4]

That last statement is where I find my batteries charged when I hear the words, "He descended into hell." I understand the woman who said that this was the *most* meaningful affirmation in the entire creed for her, because this statement told her, "He has been where I live every day." Perhaps enough people have said that (or words to that effect) when my current *Presbyterian Hymnal* was published, those who made such decisions chose *not* to footnote these words as optional.

Carlos Wilton, who has been mentioned before in this volume, is one of my dear friends, a Presbyterian pastor and wonderful preacher from New Jersey who knows his own version of hell as he battles non-Hodgkins lymphoma. Carl tells of a minister who went fishing with several of his parishioners on a lake in Oklahoma. It was the middle of the night, the hour when the most determined fishermen stalk their quarry — and everyone but the minister seemed to be catching something. Finally, he asked one of his comrades for advice.

"That lure you are using is no good," the fisherman said. "It is too bright and shiny. You need a dark one." Then the man pulled out a black lure and gave it to him.

It is night, the minister thought to himself, *what possible good is a black lure? How could the fish even see it?*

The fisherman, reading his thoughts, explained: "It is the moon. Tonight is a full moon, and that moonlight shimmers down through the waters — but it is still not bright, like the sun. A shiny lure, like you would use in the daytime, will not work at night; but a black lure stands out in silhouette against the moon."[5]

There are seasons of life when the bright optimism of good times will not do. At times like those, only a black lure, a silhouette, will succeed. We find our comfort in a Lord who was himself "crucified, dead, and buried; [who] descended into hell."

For some, the life that is a "living hell" is obvious to all. Innocent civilians caught in the crossfire of war. Starving children in Africa who are denied food and medicine simply because of the tribe into which they were born. Masses of oppressed people all around the globe whose lives are stripped of dignity, denied freedom, and living in constant fear. Because of them, we know a bit more about hell.

You may be in your own hell right now. Perhaps it is an addiction — alcohol or drugs — hell. Perhaps it is a relationship, one that started with all the promise of springtime now struggling to survive the bleakness of winter — hell. Perhaps it is some physical infirmity — the sore that will not heal that sends a message you are scared to death to hear; perhaps it is the pain that persists and pervades and allows no relief — hell. Perhaps it is an emotional state — the landscape of life is utterly bleak, and nothing that you or anyone else does is able to brighten it — hell.

Is there a hint there of what we have in Jesus? "He descended into hell," we say — even yours. As the psalmist said, in the phrasing of the venerable King James Version of scripture, "If I ascend up into heaven, thou art there: if I make my bed in hell, behold, thou art there" (Psalm 139:8). Perhaps there he can remind you that neither his story nor yours ends here. You see, the creed continues. The next word is ... *resurrection.*

"I believe ... He descended into hell. The third day he arose ..." — hallelujah!

1. "Hell: The Fear and Fascination," Rob Wallace, Producer, *20/20*, 7/13/07.

2. Jonathan Edwards, "Sinners in the Hands of Angry God," presented in Enfield, Massachusetts, 1741.

3. http://spanish.about.com/library/words/blword.htm.

4. William Barclay, *Daily Study Bible Series*, CD-ROM edition (Liguori, Missouri: Liguori Faithware, 1996). Used by permission of Westminster/John Knox Press.

5. Carlos E. Wilton, "Through The Darkest Valley," unpublished sermon, delivered at Point Pleasant Presbyterian Church, Point Pleasant, New Jersey, March 31, 1996.

Questions For Reflection

1. Does your church "go to hell"? Has there ever been any conversation about why or why not?

2. How would you describe hell?

3. The Bible has more than one description of hell (lake of fire, outer darkness, and so forth). What do you make of the various images?

4. Why do you think the concept of hell is so fascinating to people?

5. The traditional Christian understanding of hell is a place of unending torment where all those who do not profess faith in Christ will spend eternity. Do you believe that? Why or why not?

Chapter 7

He Rose Again

"I believe in God, the Father almighty, maker of heaven and earth, and in Jesus Christ his only Son our Lord, who was conceived by the Holy Ghost, born of the Virgin Mary, suffered under Pontius Pilate, was crucified, dead, and buried. He descended into hell. The third day he rose again from the dead."

I once heard of a Sunday school teacher who had just finished telling her third graders about how Jesus was crucified and placed in a tomb with a great stone sealing off the only way in or out. Then, wanting to share the excitement of the resurrection, and the surprise of Easter morning, she asked: "And what do you think were Jesus' first words when he came bursting out of that tomb alive?"

A hand shot up into the air from the rear of the classroom. It belonged to a most excited little girl. Leaping out of her chair she shouted out excitedly, "I know, I know, I know!"

"Good," said the teacher, "tell us."

Extending her arms high in the air she sang out: "Ta-da!"

Wow! Put yourself in the place of those who heard about it first. They knew what had happened. They were eyewitnesses, albeit from a distance. The arrest, the trial, the torture, the murder — and murder it surely was. Jesus was dead, dead as a doornail. If the crucifixion had not done him in, that spear through the side had settled the issue.

After the horror was over, a caring friend named Joseph, of the town of Arimathea (which is no longer on any map), requested of Pilate that he be granted Jesus' body for burial. Pilate acceded to the request, the remains were removed from the cross, wrapped in a white linen shroud, and laid in Joseph's own new tomb. A large stone was rolled in front of the entrance to prevent unwanted intrusion.

There were still issues though. The religious leaders who had instigated the crucifixion came to Pilate and reminded the governor what Jesus had said.

65

Sir, we remember that while he was still alive that deceiver said, "After three days I will rise again." So give the order for the tomb to be made secure until the third day. Otherwise, his disciples may come and steal the body and tell the people that he has been raised from the dead. This last deception will be worse than the first. — Matthew 27:63-64

No problem. Pilate assigned some soldiers to guard the tomb and seal that stone.

The body lay there from Friday evening until Sunday morning, three days, by Jewish reckoning. And then suddenly, the tomb is empty, the body gone — Ta-da!

How is that possible? Perhaps he was not really dead to start with. Perhaps he only went into a deep swoon on the cross and regained consciousness while in the cool damp of the borrowed tomb. He awoke, got up, rolled the stone away, and walked off. Right past the Roman guards, men for whom falling asleep at their post was a capital offense. Uh-huh. As badly beaten up and wounded as Jesus was, having lost an incredible amount of blood, having gone without food or water for several days, and as dangerous as it would have been for those legionnaires, that requires more of a leap of faith than coming back from the dead.

Perhaps some wild dogs got in there and ate the corpse — gruesome, but not unheard of in those days. Still, those would have had to be some incredibly fastidious animals, not leaving even a shred of meat or bone or hair on the floor for someone to notice. And which of the dogs would have folded the cloth that had covered Jesus' head, rolled it and laid it carefully to one side — one of them must have done it, because that is what Peter and John found when they came into the tomb (John 20:7). Those would be very talented dogs and another leap of faith.

Of course, there is the possibility that Jesus' friends came to the wrong tomb. As the ladies came into the garden at dawn on the first day of the week, their grief had so disoriented them that they went to the wrong place, jumped to a hasty conclusion, then ran back to tell the others. That would also mean that Peter and John would have been equally directionally challenged because they certainly could have and happily *would* have corrected the ladies in their error, if they had made one.

One more obvious possibility — the one that the religious leaders tried to disseminate. Jesus' friends had simply stolen the body, reburied it in some secret location, and began to circulate this incredible tale of resurrection, the stone miraculously rolled away, strange angelic beings saying things like, "Why do you look for the living among the dead? He is not here; he has risen!" (Luke 24:5b-6a). Amazingly, for folks who were pulling a gigantic hoax, this is the story they would *all* stick to, everyone of them, without anyone ever breaking ranks, and that would finally cost most of them their lives. Was it a hoax?

You know, for me it takes less faith to believe that Jesus was raised from the dead than to believe any of those stories that would try to explain the miraculous event away. "I believe ... the third day he rose again from the dead."

Do you believe it? Really? John Killinger suggests that we have three possible answers to that question:

1. It did not happen. It is merely a fiction invented by the early church.
2. It did happen, and therefore we do not understand the world we live in as well as we thought we did.
3. It did happen, but only because there is a Power so great that it can contravene the laws of the world as we know it.[1]

Now, from the viewpoint of those closest to Jesus, it did happen. There can be no doubt about that. They knew that people do not normally revive after they have died — especially after three days. This is why they reacted as they did. Running hither and thither, like chickens with their heads cut off.

Will Willimon tells the story of a boy in his high school chemistry class. During some experiment gone wrong, there was an explosion in the back of the room. Nothing serious, just a loud bang. And this young lad, seated at the front, bolted out the door, ran down the hall, and was not heard from again that day.

"What on earth were you thinking about?" the teacher asked him the next day.

"I wasn't thinking about anything," he said. "I was just running. I didn't know what to do, so I ran."[2]

Mary, what were you thinking about when you found the tomb empty and heard the angel say, "Do not be afraid; I know that you are looking for Jesus who was crucified. He is not here; for he has been raised, as he said. Come, see the place where he lay." What were you thinking, Mary?

"I did not know what to think, so I just ran."

Peter, John, what were you thinking when the women came to you with the report of the empty tomb?

"What *could* we think, besides the fact that they were probably crazy? We just ran."

We know what they found.

Did the resurrection occur as we have always heard? I say, "Yes." There are four major pieces of evidence. First, there was the empty tomb. No fewer than four followers saw the empty tomb and reported it. We have already noted the attempts to explain that away, but, in my view, none are in the least compelling.

Second, there were all the appearances of the risen Christ — to Mary in the garden; to two disciples on the road to Emmaus; to ten of the disciples in the upper room; to those ten again, plus Thomas a week later; to several disciples by the Sea of Galilee; and then to more than 500 followers at once.

Third, there was the incredible change in the attitudes and behavior of the followers. Before the crucifixion, they acted from cowardice and confusion. After the resurrection, they were transformed into pillars of power; they were courageous and decisive, ready to die for their faith. The same Peter who, in saving his own skin, had denied he even knew Jesus, just weeks later would stand on a balcony in the heart of Jerusalem and boldly proclaim,

> *You that are Israelites, listen to what I have to say: Jesus of Nazareth, a man attested to you by God with deeds of power, wonders, and signs that God did through him among you, as you yourselves know — this man, handed*

over to you according to the definite plan and foreknowledge of God, you crucified and killed by the hands of those outside the law. But God raised him up, having freed him from death, because it was impossible for him to be held in its power. — Acts 2:22-24 (NRSV)

Something had happened to Peter. Something had happened to all of them. Something changed them — and we know what it was.

Fourth, there is the very existence of the church. These friends of Jesus — faithful, monotheistic Jews, every one — had been raised with the understanding that one thing and one thing alone cemented their identity before the world as the people of God — the observance of the sabbath. Now, they begin a tradition of worship on the first day of the week instead of the seventh. They took this extraordinary step of changing the holy day from Saturday to Sunday and calling it *the Lord's day*. Only a mind-boggling event could have been responsible for such a shift. And we know what that event was: "The third day he rose again from the dead."

So saying, there are still questions to which we have no answers. Scripture never tells us *how* Jesus was resurrected, just that it happened. And what about Christ's resurrection body? It appears to be the same as before but there must be something different. It could pass through locked doors unhindered. In almost every account, Jesus is not recognized at first — not by Mary, not by the two disciples going to Emmaus, nor by the bigger groups of disciples gathered in the upper room and beside the sea. Why? I do not know.

Killinger suggests that we opt for one of three possibilities: it did not happen; it happened, but we do not understand; it happened because divine power *made* it happen. For me, I would like to opt for both the second and the third. I admit I do not fully understand the nature of the world we live in, and I am convinced that God intervened in an unusual way to rescue Jesus from the grave. "I believe ... the third day he rose again from the dead."

And I believe one more thing. I believe Jesus was telling the truth when he said, "Because I live, you also will live" (John 14:19).

Throughout our study we have been insisting that as we believe, so we behave. What difference does our belief in Jesus' resurrection make? Primarily this: Death is not the final word — not for him — not for us. That means we never need fear death again, for we know that death is not a period but a comma, not the end, but the beginning.

It was just after midnight on Saturday night. I was putting the wraps on the next morning's message and the telephone rang. It was the police. They were calling to let me know the awful news about Ashley, a wonderful fourteen-year-old who had just been killed in an automobile accident. By the time folks gathered for worship the next morning, word had spread. Most of us were in shock. Most of us were in tears.

When it came time for worship, I scrapped the sermon I had prepared and instead shared a word that tried to convey my own belief that, even in the face of the worst that life slams our way, there is still hope — all this is ultimately in the hands of a God who loved us so much that Jesus came and died that we might live. The word was not that *because* everything is so wonderful, I believe. No. The word was everything is *not* wonderful; *nevertheless*, I believe.

Alas, the weekend was not over. After church we headed to the hospital. Dear Mildred, 67 years old, was very near death after a long and arduous bout with cancer. Mildred had been a wonderful friend to my family and me from the time we arrived in that community. I had visited Mildred in the hospital on many occasions before this. She had been an in-patient at least a dozen times in the two years I had known her. This time I would not be going alone though — my family wanted to go, too. My daughter, especially. Somehow, those two had become incredibly close — a 67-year-old and a 10-year-old — girlfriends. They went shopping together and had pajama parties. She called Mildred her "God-Grandmother." On the night table beside her bed was one picture: her pal, Mildred. Now, the end was near — Mildred would be going home very soon.

An hour went by, then another and another. I left the hospital to go visit Ashley's family. My family stayed. I came back to the hospital. There was no change. "It's getting late; don't you want to go home, sweetie?" I said to my daughter.

"No. I don't want to go home until Mildred goes home."

Finally, about 7:30 that evening, with still no change and no indication when one might come, She agreed to leave. We had been home only a few minutes when the call came to let us know. It was over.

There was a certain amount of sanctified speculation that followed. The Bible gives us few details about the transition from earth to heaven, so there was wondering if Ashley and Mildred might run into each other in whatever "celestial lobby" there might be. "Fancy meeting you here." "And you, too." Could they have encountered one another while standing in line waiting for assignments, directions, wings, whatever? Nah. Any of you who has ever been in the service or gone through a college registration knows that standing in line is hell, not heaven. So....

Now there were two funerals to prepare and within a few hours there would be a third. This one not for a member of the church but a friend for whom I had provided pastoral care in recent months and who had now succumbed after a long and painful illness. As every preacher knows, "It comes with the territory." Like it or not.

The heart of my faith insists that this life is not all there is. One reason I believe, I admit, is that at a very deep level, I want to. Faith grows out of a subsoil of yearning, and something instinctive in human beings cries out against the reign of death. Whether hope takes the form of Egyptian pharaohs stashing their jewels and chariots in pyramids, or the modern American obsession with keeping bodies alive until the last possible second regardless of how much suffering comes with it, we humans resist the idea of death having the final say. We want to believe otherwise.

And we do. Thus our affirmation, "I believe ... the third day, he rose again from the dead."

71

1. Killinger, *You Are What You Believe: The Apostles' Creed For Today* (Nashville: Abingdon, 1990), p. 67.

2. William Willimon, "Getting to Easter," 3/30/97, via internet, http://www.chapel.duke.edu/sermons/MAR30SER.htm.

Questions For Reflection

1. We have heard the story of the resurrection so often that it no longer shocks or surprises us. Is that a positive or a negative?

2. Is there anything that is particularly striking about the behavior of Christ's followers after the resurrection?

3. What are some barriers to belief in Christ's resurrection?

4. Paul says in 1 Corinthians 15 that without Christ's resurrection our faith is in vain. Why?

5. If death is not the final word for us, should Christians grieve at the loss of a loved one?

Chapter 8

He Ascended

"I believe in God, the Father almighty, maker of heaven and earth, and in Jesus Christ his only Son our Lord, who was conceived by the Holy Ghost, born of the Virgin Mary, suffered under Pontius Pilate, was crucified, dead, and buried. He descended into hell. The third day he rose again from the dead. He ascended into heaven, and sitteth on the right hand of God the Father almighty."

"He ascended ..." — up, up, and away. It must have been a very strange sensation for those on the hillside. What was this? A magic show? Jesus suddenly levitating above them, disappearing into a cloud? What's the trick? Is David Copperfield around here someplace? Okay, you can bring him back. Anyway, we have work to do. A kingdom to establish. Besides, we were not done talking. What did he mean, "John baptized with water, but you will be baptized with the Holy Spirit not many days from now"? (Acts 1:5 NRSV). And what was that about, "You will receive power when the Holy Spirit has come upon you; and you will be my witnesses in Jerusalem, in all Judea and Samaria, and to the ends of the earth"? Come back, Jesus, the show is over. Come back — Jesus ... Jesus? But he was gone.

You have probably heard this apocryphal story before. Jesus arrives at the pearly gates following the ascension. The angel host was gathered to welcome God's Son and celebrate his return home after his incredible sojourn on earth. Everyone had questions and wanted to hear his story — born of a virgin, raised in humble circumstances, years teaching, preaching, and healing. Eventually, there was that gruesome torture and murder, but finally the conquest of humanity's most feared enemy — death. All to share the good news of a loving God who wants nothing but the best for creation. Now the Christ is *home*, and everyone is exultant.

Someone asks, "Lord, now that you are no longer physically on earth, who will continue to share the good news?"

Christ responds, "There are eleven who were especially close to me, and I have given them the responsibility of getting the word out."

"O Lord, these eleven must be incredible people — the best and the brightest that creation has to offer!"

"Well, actually, no," the Lord responds. "These are average folks with ordinary abilities. Not the 'best and the brightest' by any means."

"But Lord, if these are only average people with ordinary ability, how can you be sure that they will get the job done?"

"Well, to be honest," the Lord answers, "I can't be sure."

"You cannot be sure, Lord? Well, what if they fail to do the job? What is your backup plan?"

Quietly Christ answers, "I have no backup plan."

Hmm.

One might figure that our friends would be depressed at Jesus' disappearance. After all, they had been on quite an emotional roller coaster. There were the good times traveling through the countryside for three years, the bad times of trial and torture that culminated at Calvary, the good times together once more following the resurrection, now ... gone again. Who could blame them for being dejected? The record says, "a cloud hid him from their sight." Hmm ... the same cloud that led the children of Israel in the wilderness? Good Jews had long looked at clouds as symbolic of the presence of God. Perhaps that is why, instead of dismay and depression, in the other biblical account of the ascension in Luke's gospel (Luke 24:51-53), we find the disciples returning to Jerusalem "with great joy." Somehow, they understood that Jesus had simply gone home.

He had stated over and over again that this was the plan (John 14:2, 12; 16:5, 28; 20:17; and so forth). This was not, "Good-bye," but rather, "See you later." He said, "In my Father's house are many rooms; if it were not so, I would have told you. I am going there to prepare a place for you. And if I go and prepare a place for you, I will come back and take you to be with me that you also may be where I am" (John 14:2-3). This was not the end of their relationship with Jesus but a brand new beginning. Not a cause for despair but case for delight!

In a unique way, their Lord and Savior was not *less* accessible but *more*. No longer would he be limited by space and time, but now would be available *every*where and *any*time by the presence of his Holy Spirit. Within just days and weeks, that pitiful band of beleaguered believers, which had hidden itself behind locked doors in fear for its life stood boldly in the public arena and proclaimed the gospel of the crucified and risen Christ. It spread beyond Jerusalem, just as Jesus said, into Judea and Samaria and on to the ends of the earth. What a difference! It gave rise to the first confession of faith the church ever had: *Jesus Christ is Lord!* It is fleshed out by what we repeat from week to week: "He ascended into heaven and sitteth on the right hand of God the Father almighty." What glory!

The great Christian missionary to India, E. Stanley Jones, a close friend of Mahatma Gandhi, commented that after Gandhi's assassination, the radio constantly broadcast programs that eulogized the father of that great land. He noted that a Mrs. Naidu, a well-known Hindu poet, spoke on Sunday, three days after the assassination. She had been in frequent contact with the Christian community in India, and her words carried an eloquence born of her emotion: "O Bapu, O Little Father, come back. We are orphaned without you. We are lost without you. Come back and lead us."

Jones said he could sympathize with her plea, representing the cry of a stricken nation. As he sat there he thought, "O God, I am grateful I do not have to cry that cry for the leader of my soul: 'O Jesus, come back. Come back. We are orphaned and stricken without you.'" He knew that his master had been received in glory, that he is a living presence in our lives day by day, and that he is coming back to redeem the entire world.[1] "He ascended into heaven and sitteth on the right hand of God the Father almighty."

The point of the whole matter, of course, is a reminder of who Jesus is — not simply some ancient itinerant rabbi who taught timeless truths, not simply some helpful Hebrew healer who had remarkable power over disease and even death, not simply a compassionate, caring friend who reached out to those whom society rejected, but rather the God of all creation come to earth, incarnate in human flesh. Now it was time for his return to glory.

The early scribe who, blessed with divine wisdom, completed the Lord's Prayer for oral repetition by adding the resounding phrase, "for thine is the kingdom, the power, and the glory" knew what he was doing. It was the perfect touch. That scribe knew from the depths of his being, Jesus "ascended into heaven and sitteth on the right hand of God the Father almighty."

We have strong biblical warrant for that statement. It starts with Psalm 110: "The Lord says to my Lord: 'Sit at my right hand until I make your enemies a footstool for your feet' " (v. 1). Jesus quotes it. Paul quotes it. Peter quotes it. "... you will see the Son of Man sitting at the right hand of the Mighty One ..." (Mark 14:62), says Jesus. He is "exalted to the right hand of God" (Acts 2:33), says Peter in his sermon on the day of Pentecost. "Look, I see heaven open and the Son of Man standing at the right hand of God" (Acts 7:56), says Stephen just before being stoned to death. "Who is he that condemns?" asks Paul. "Christ Jesus, who died — more than that, who was raised to life — is at the right hand of God and is also interceding for us" (Romans 8:34).

First Peter speaks of "Jesus Christ, who has gone into heaven and is at God's right hand — with angels, authorities and powers in submission to him" (3:21-22). And the writer to the Hebrews: "After he had provided purification for sins, he sat down at the right hand of the Majesty in heaven" (1:3). This was the position of honor; this was the place of power; this was where King Jesus belonged through all the ages. Glory!

He deserved it. True, he wrote no books, composed no songs, drew no pictures, carved no statues, amassed no fortune, commanded no army, ruled no nation. Yet, he who never wrote a line has been made the hero of unnumbered volumes. He who never wrote a song has put music into the hearts of nameless multitudes. He who never established an institution is the foundation of the church that bears his name. He who refused the kingdoms of this world has become the Lord of millions. Yes, he whose shameful death scarcely produced a ripple on the pool of history in his day has become a mighty current in the vast ocean of the centuries since he died.[2]

Recently, several toy manufacturers have decided to tap into the "faith market" by producing biblically based dolls and action figures. Whether they will be successful or not only time will tell. So saying, they might recall what happened a half-century ago when Ben Michtom, president of the Ideal Toy Company, had a brainstorm: Why not sell a Jesus doll? In 1957, the majority of children in America were Christian, so he figured parents would jump at the opportunity to make playtime a religious experience. Other Ideal executives were horrified, but Michtom was convinced it was a great idea. To prove it, he took his case to a higher authority; while on vacation in Italy, he got an audience with the pope and pitched the idea to him. The pope gave his blessing, as did every other Christian leader Michtom consulted.

Unfortunately for Ideal, Michtom did not consult any parents, who probably would have told him the idea was a loser (which it turned out to be). As Sydney Stem describes the doll in *Toyland, The High-Stakes Game of the Toy Industry*,[3] no one bought them because parents were horrified at the idea of undressing the Jesus doll, dragging it around, sticking it in the bathtub. Nothing sold. Ordinarily, there is a no-return policy on products already shipped. But in this case it was such a horrible mistake that Ideal took them back. It appears that what Ideal did with them was give each of its employees a doll and then they ground up the rest and put them in landfills.

Jesus dolls — packaged in a box that looked like the Bible — were probably the biggest doll flop in American toy history.[4] Why? Because even though people of faith celebrate the fact that Jesus was truly human — walked, talked, ate, drank, suffered, even died — we know there is more to his story: "He rose again from the dead. He ascended into heaven and sitteth at the right hand of God the Father almighty." That is not dollhouse stuff!

So saying, there is something utterly unique with this king: Instead of being draped with the trappings of an all-powerful potentate as he deserves, he reigns as a suffering servant. Our sovereign Lord is revealed in the one who walked the dusty roads of Palestine, who had no place to lay his head, who emptied himself in obedience all the way to the cross. That was not the end of the story, of course. Hallelujah — he who died to be our Savior now lives to be our Lord. "He ascended into heaven and sitteth on the right hand of God the Father almighty."

Do you believe it? We continue to insist, as we believe, so we behave. How do we behave in honoring such a cosmic king as Christ? A good start is by taking his instructions seriously. If you want a quick primer on acceptable behavior, take a fast trip through the Sermon on the Mount (Matthew 5-7). Angry words, insulting words, are out. Our sexual behavior will be in control. We will be honest in our business dealings. We will go above and beyond the call of duty in response to appeals for help. We will care for the welfare of, not only our neighbor, but our enemy as well. We will be religious, but not showy about it. Possessions will have their rightful place in our lives, not the be-all and end-all of existence. We will not be judgmental, but we will use good judgment. We will trust God to meet our needs. Of course, the gospels have much more for us, but those should do to get us started. Is Jesus Christ your Lord? Good — then you will do your level best to do what he says.

Piece of cake, eh? Of course not, but we have the promise of his abiding presence to help us on our journey. This is, after all, our *living* Lord, the same one who "ascended into heaven and sitteth at the right hand of God the Father almighty." This is the one who is ultimately in charge, and that, my friend, is a wonderful word of hope for you or me or anyone who has ever been drenched in the storms of life. It is a word of hope for this old world that says "the wrong shall fail, the right prevail."

Quietly now. Listen for it. Faintly to be heard over the din of police whistles and fire sirens, the whine of fighter-bombers and missiles, the anguished cries of the mothers of murdered children, you can begin to make it out. "He ascended into heaven and sitteth at the right hand of God the Father Almighty." Slowly but surely it builds to crescendo: "The kingdoms of this world have become the kingdom of our Lord and of his Christ. And he shall reign forever and ever. Hallelujah!"

1. John Killinger, *You Are What You Believe: The Apostles' Creed for Today* (Nashville: Abingdon, 1990), p. 76.

2. Mack Stokes quoted by James S. Hewett, *Illustrations Unlimited* (Wheaton, Illinois: Tyndale House Publishers, Inc, 1988), p. 73.

3. Sydney Stem, *Toyland, The High-Stakes Game of the Toy Industry* (Chicago: Contemporary Books, 1990).

4. Dynamic Illustrations quoting *Uncle John's Ultimate Bathroom Reader* (Berkeley, California: The Bathroom Readers' Institute, Bathroom Readers' Press, 1996).

Questions For Reflection

1. How are we to understand the "right hand of God" imagery that we find in reference to the ascended Christ?

2. The descriptions of the heavenly throne room should probably best be understood poetically rather than photographically. Are there other instances in scripture where we find something similar?

3. Of Christ's priorities that we find in the gospels, which are the most problematic in our day?

4. Is the Sermon on the Mount a good primer for Christian behavior? Are there others?

5. Will the recently introduced toys for the "faith market" do any better today than the Jesus doll did in 1957? Why?

Chapter 9

He Shall Come To Judge

"I believe in God, the Father almighty, maker of heaven and earth, and in Jesus Christ his only Son our Lord, who was conceived by the Holy Ghost, born of the Virgin Mary, suffered under Pontius Pilate, was crucified, dead, and buried. He descended into hell. The third day he rose again from the dead. He ascended into heaven, and sitteth on the right hand of God the Father almighty. From thence he shall come to judge the quick and the dead."

Judgment — a disquieting thought. Ever been to court? Most of us have, at one time or another. How did you feel when you went into the courtroom? I cannot speak for anyone else, but every time I have set foot in one of those august chambers, looking toward the raised bench from which sentence would be passed, I have been a bit awe-struck. "Oyez, oyez, oyez," intones the bailiff in calling for order and inviting those with business to draw near. The judge is introduced — "All rise!" — and a black-robed figure bustles in and takes the chair behind the lofty bench. "God bless the United States of America and God bless this honorable court. Be seated." That is very awesome.

Now move that scene up exponentially — the picture painted in Revelation. The entire universe is transformed into a courtroom and everyone who ever lived has been subpoenaed there. Presiding over the proceedings from a lofty bench is the Lord of all creation. Amidst the shuffling and shifting, the papers are arranged and the books are opened. "Call the first case." Awesome.

Is that how it will be ... at the end of time? Hard to say. After all, the pictures we get throughout the book of Revelation are more poetic than photographic. What we *can* and *do* say is that "I believe ... [Jesus will] come again to judge the quick and the dead."

A brief word on the language here. "The quick and the dead" refers not to pedestrians trying to cross a busy street at rush hour where one had better be quick or else end up dead. The "quick" of our affirmation is simply Elizabethan English for "living" or "alive."

The point of what we say is that no one escapes this process. Even death is no escape.

Is that what you believe? Jesus is coming and will judge? Have you thought about it? From conversations I have had with parishioners over the years, many *have* considered the question, but despite the fact that week in and week out we say "from thence he shall come to judge the quick and the dead," there is not much clarity about the affirmation.

Break it in two. Consider just "He shall come." Scripture says so. In the upper room with his disciples, Jesus himself said he was going away but promised to come again (John 14:3). At his ascension, the two angels declared, "This same Jesus, who has been taken from you into heaven, will come back in the same way you have seen him go into heaven" (Acts 1:11). There are all those bumper stickers declaring, "In the event of the Rapture, this car will have no driver." Those refer to a portion of a letter that Paul wrote to the church at Thessalonica.

> *For the Lord himself will come down from heaven, with a loud command, with the voice of the archangel and with the trumpet call of God, and the dead in Christ will rise first. After that, we who are still alive and are left will be caught up together with them in the clouds to meet the Lord in the air. And so we will be with the Lord forever.* — 1 Thessalonians 4:16-17

Whether we are to understand that literally is open to question. Regardless, it is one more biblical affirmation of Christ's second coming.

I heard much about that as I was growing up. Perhaps you did, too. Mostly, it was shared as a way of keeping sinful teenagers in line (and I suspect that has been the case for every generation for almost 2,000 years): "Do not be caught somewhere or with someone or doing something which would be an embarrassment if the Lord should come back right then and see you." And there was the reminder that the second coming could be at any moment, so be ready! Did the warnings work? Well....

Is the Lord coming back? As I say, scripture says so, and so do we from week to week: "from thence he shall come...." But, so saying, the return might not be in the way that traditional understanding has taught (and I can promise it will not be the cause of massive traffic accidents because of driverless vehicles — what kind of God would cause such a mess?). So saying, I am satisfied to leave the details in the Lord's hands. I am content to know that, one day, whether individually at the end of my earthly journey or as one of a great band of believers at the end of history, he is coming for me, and I will see him face-to-face.

Now, what about the second half of our affirmation? "To judge the quick and the dead?" How are we to understand God's judgment? Again, the concept is thoroughly biblical. In the Old Testament God's judgment is demonstrated concerning nations, their rulers, and individuals. In the New Testament, divine judgment is a both a *present* reality ... John's gospel: "This is the verdict: Light has come into the world, but men loved darkness instead of light because their deeds were evil" (3:19) ... and a *future* certainty ... John again: "a time is coming when all who are in their graves will hear his voice and come out — those who have done good will rise to live, and those who have done evil will rise to be condemned" (5:28-29). In the scene we encounter in Revelation, the basis of judgment is both from the book of life and also from the books of works.

Here is where questions come. Some ask if Christians go through the judgment just like everyone else. After all, it was Jesus himself who said, "I tell you the truth, whoever hears my word and believes him who sent me has eternal life and will not be condemned; he has crossed over from death to life" (John 5:24). The issue is eternal destiny — for believers, it is settled and, as scripture affirms, is not a subject for judgment.

The story does not end there — there is that matter of this judgment of our works. I know, I know, I know — we who are the heirs of the Reformation have a fit on that one. Were we not always taught by the apostle Paul, "For it is by grace you have been saved, through faith — and this not from yourselves, it is the gift of God — not by works, so that no one can boast" (Ephesians 2:8-9)? True enough. But Paul also taught, "For we must all appear before the judgment seat of Christ, that each one may receive what is due him for the things done while in the body, whether good or bad" (2 Corinthians 5:10). He talked about the quality of our works — some terrific, as if gold, silver, or precious stones, others not so terrific, in quality like nothing more than wood, hay, or stubble. Come the day of judgment, the good stuff survives and is even refined, but the bad is just wiped out, gone in a puff of smoke. The worker is saved, but the works are gone (1 Corinthians 3:12-15).

So the question comes again: Are believers subject to judgment? And that wonderful answer is, "Yes," and "No." *No*, concerning our destiny; *yes*, concerning our behavior. "From thence he shall come to judge the quick and the dead" ... *all* of them, you and me included.

I remember an occasion of being in court in North Carolina. Our son had gotten a traffic ticket. I had gone down to Charlotte to bring him home from college for the weekend. He was the driver for the return trip. Passing by Salisbury, a state trooper pulled him over. He may have been exceeding the limit a little bit, but he was keeping with the flow of traffic and not driving unsafely. If he had been, I would have been giving him more grief than any officer, because, as he would be the first to attest, I can be one of the world's most vocal and vehement backseat drivers. We thought and thought about what might have caught the trooper's attention, and the only thing I could figure was, at some point, as we traveled cheek-by-jowl at highway speed with an eighteen-wheeler five feet from my face, I probably said, "Get past this guy." He did, and the blue lights began to flash. For the first time in his life, he was pulled over.

"License and registration, please." My son handed them over. The trooper took them back to his cruiser, did whatever troopers do in such situations, then came back with a ticket. He was being charged with exceeding the speed limit in a work zone and fined $230! He could mail the money in and be done with it, or he could dispute it. $230? The punishment did not fit the crime. We would take this one to court. There was a preliminary appearance to determine if we might accept a lesser plea. Our answer was, "No," and the date was set.

We arrived at the courthouse early, the first ones there. We had been told that cases were arranged with order of arrival taken into account (and such is apparently the case in preliminary appearances), but early, schm-early, on this day it made no difference. We took our seats in the criminal court amidst a packed house. Case after case was called. Drug dealers, wife-beaters, petty thieves — this was not the "cream of society" forming the passing parade but rather the curdled milk. Hour after hour we watched and waited. The judge was impressive: fair, open, tough when he needed to be, merciful when that appeared called for. He was sharp. Recess for lunch. More watching and waiting. Hour melted into hour as the crowd slowly dwindled. The courtroom was almost empty now. The biblical irony was not wasted on us — "the first shall be last," and we were. The last case of the day.

My son had prepared his defense. There may have been a breach of the speed limit, but it was not in a work zone despite the charge, and thus should not be subject to an outrageously high fine. He had drafted a careful diagram of the scene to demonstrate the contention. He had driven to Raleigh for an official copy of his heretofore unstained driving record. Suddenly, he was being asked to play Perry Mason. This was formal. Witnesses were sworn. The district attorney examined the trooper. When it came to the cross-examination we heard, "And *you* have to do this son, not your father."

Gulp! "Uh, no questions, your honor."

It was my son's turn. He took the stand himself. In his hand he held the painstakingly prepared diagram, which the court examined with care. He offered his recollection of events and answered questions from the judge.

"All right, son, stand down," said the judge as he continued to look at the diagram. "How long have you been driving?"

"Three-and-a-half years, your honor."

"Have you ever had a ticket before?"

"No sir. My record is spotless." He approached the bench and handed over the copy of his driving history. The judge smiled at the forcefulness of the answer.

87

With the evidence at hand, the judge was not comfortable declaring him "not guilty," but he was not going to convict either. "Prayer for judgment," he said (the North Carolina equivalent of probation without verdict). "Pay the court costs, and slow down when you are passing Salisbury on your way home from school."

Hallelujah!

That story is a parable. You see, when it comes to passing judgment, more is involved than rendering a sentence. A good judge is going to do his or her level best to have things come out *right* for all concerned. Our judge that day did. The judge of all the earth whom we meet in the pages of scripture is no different.

You see, in the biblical tradition, "judgment" is not primarily punishment; it is the restoration of order; it is setting right a situation that has gone wrong. When we affirm our faith in a final judgment, we are trusting the divine judge to fix things. Listen to the way our Southern Presbyterian "Declaration of Faith" put it a few years ago:

> *All things will be renewed in Christ ...*
> *As he stands at the center of our history,*
> *we are confident he will stand at its end.*
> *He will judge all people and nations.*
> *Evil will be condemned*
> *and rooted out of God's good creation.*
> *There will be no more tears or pain.*
> *All things will be made new.*
> *The fellowship of human beings*
> *with God and each other will be perfected.*

Again, we reach for our anchor in this series of messages: "As we believe, so we behave." What does our affirmation about final judgment mean to us?

My friend, Al Winn, suggests that since this is the way it is going to be ultimately and finally — perfect — let us begin now. Let us tell the truth now. Let us stop playing games with each other now. If we are to be judged by how we have treated the least of these, Christ's brothers and sisters, let us begin now to reevaluate who is important. Let us approximate justice now. Let us practice compassion now. Let us stop worrying so much about what people think and what people may say and what the newspaper may publish now. Let us ask what the judge will think and what the judge will say. Let us ask now.

Dr. Winn recalls a friend who was a pastor in South Carolina at the height of the Civil Rights struggle. One of his members came to him, very upset, to ask why he preached so much about justice to black people. "Because," the pastor said, "I believe in the last judgment. In that day you will know the truth. You will understand clearly that the way you treat powerless people is the way you treat Jesus Christ himself. And when all that hits you, I don't want you to look across at me, your pastor, and ask, 'Why didn't you tell me?' I want to be clear of your blood."

"Do you really believe in the last judgment?" asked the man.

"Literally," said his pastor.[1]

So do we, we say. "From thence he shall come to judge the quick and the dead."

_____

1. Albert Curry Winn, *A Christian Primer: The Prayer, The Creed, The Commandments* (Louisville: Westminster/John Knox Press, 1990), p. 150.

Questions For Reflection

1. If you were the judge, for what would you reserve the harshest judgment? Do you think Jesus would agree?

2. Christians have preached and taught that the Lord would return again and soon, but that has not happened for 2,000 years. Should the message be revisited?

3. Will you as an individual be judged more harshly on the things you have done or the things you have failed to do?

4. If the church is responsible for telling the good news of the gospel, how responsible is the church for issuing warnings about judgment?

5. When you come to that eternal moment of judgment, do you want justice or mercy?

Chapter 10

The Holy Ghost

"I believe in the Holy Ghost...."

An old story. A group of children lived near a cemetery that was situated around a suburban church. They would often play near a hedge adjacent to the graves and, while there, hear the ministers conducting services. One day they played funerals and dug a grave in which they buried a pretend casket. One of them intoned the prayers and ended with what he assumed the minister was saying: "In the name of the father, and of the son, and in the hole he goes!"

Do you believe in ghosts? Do you? Be careful how you respond. After all, from week to week we say, "I believe in the Holy Ghost," even though many folks might have no more understanding of what they are saying than those kids at their funeral.

"I believe in the Holy Ghost." Today when we say the word "ghost" most folks mean an apparition from the dead, as in Dickens' "Ghost of Christmas Past," or "Casper the Friendly...." But 400 years ago, when our New Testament was translated from Greek into English, "ghost" was an Anglo-Saxon word which meant "spirit." For example, in the King James account of the death of Christ, we read that Jesus "gave up the ghost" (Mark 15:37, 39; Luke 23:46; John 19:30), meaning that the spirit of life left his body. So when you say you believe in the Holy Ghost what you mean is the Holy Spirit (and that is the way many modern statements of the creed render this affirmation — "I believe in the Holy Spirit").

Come to think of it, the only time we hear reference to the "Holy Ghost" outside of our creed is from our Pentecostal friends who are apparently reluctant to update the terminology. To be painfully honest, most folks in the mainline church are more than a little put off by our enthusiastic compatriots — the worship with eyes tightly closed and hands waving in the air; the seeming lack of decorum during services with their shouts of "Hallelujah,"

"Amen," and "Preach, Brother, Preach"; the speaking in tongues, the televangelists with people being knocked off their feet ("slain in the Spirit," as they say) in miracles of healing. On top of that, we get the feeling that our energetic friends look down their theological noses at us who refer to ourselves as God's "frozen chosen" because we have not arrived at their lofty level of spiritual enlightenment.

I will never forget sitting in worship as a boy, looking out over the congregation from my perch in the junior choir one Sunday as my father preached (a man who, by the way, was one of God's wonderful saints — quiet, kind, caring, and who everyone saw was utterly devoted to Jesus Christ). Suddenly a woman who was visiting for the first time stood up in the midst of the sermon and asked, "Pastor, have you spoken in tongues?" Dad responded in the gentle way that was always his and said that he had not. She retorted quickly (just before the ushers got to her) that he was obviously not much of a Christian. That sort of spiritual elitism is very uncomfortable. I for one have no interest in affirming faith in any "Holy Ghost" who would prompt such behavior.

So what then *is* this Spirit in which we say we believe? We could be wonderfully orthodox and say, "The third person in the Trinity." Or, along with John's gospel (depending on which translation is in hand), the Advocate, or the Comforter, or the Counselor. The Greek word behind those terms is *parakletos*, a term which comes from the courtroom and means one who walks along side, sort of a defense attorney, but on a deeper level, one who looks out for you — the Paraclete. In Jesus' words on that night of the Last Supper, knowing that he would soon no longer be physically present, "I will not leave you orphaned." This "Paraclete" will be as the presence of Jesus himself, reminding the faithful of all they have already been taught and teaching new lessons to meet the challenges of tomorrow.

We hear about the Holy Spirit in John's gospel, but we get to meet the Spirit in the book of Acts. Indeed, some have suggested that the title of the book should not be the Acts of the Apostles, but rather the Acts of the Holy Spirit. As the book opens, the disciples are gathered with Jesus on the Mount of Olives just prior to the

Ascension. Jesus tells them to go to Jerusalem and wait — the power of the Holy Spirit would come upon them. They went, they waited, they prayed, and *blam*! Power — Pentecost — see the way scripture describes it:

> *Suddenly a sound like the blowing of a violent wind came from heaven and filled the whole house where they were sitting. They saw what seemed to be tongues of fire that separated and came to rest on each of them. All of them were filled with the Holy Spirit and began to speak in other tongues as the Spirit enabled them.*
> — Acts 2:2-4

The story goes on. Peter, the same man who just weeks before had been so protective of his own precious hide that he had denied even knowing Jesus, now, in front of thousands of Jerusalem's Pentecost pilgrims, stands and proclaims boldly the gospel of the crucified and risen Christ. Pentecost has been called the birthday of the church because Peter's preaching was so powerful that 3,000 joined the fellowship that day. Wow!

As the story continues, we find the Spirit enabling miracles of healing, more bold proclamation in the face of opposition and even arrest. A marvelous heart of sharing began to beat in the church and leaders with gifts of compassion were empowered to oversee ministries of concern and consolation. As time would go on, others would experience spiritual gifts of their own — preaching, teaching, healing, forms of leadership, the much-misunderstood gift of tongues, and especially the gift of love.

Witness? Even in the face of death, the Spirit enabled powerful testimony. The Spirit began to move the faithful and their message beyond Jerusalem ... down on the Jericho Road as Philip shared the word of Jesus with an Ethiopian eunuch; the Damascus Road as Saul of Tarsus, one of the most zealous persecutors of the young church, was unceremoniously dumped in the dirt and marvelously converted; in Caesarea, as Peter offered the good news of the gospel and broke the racial barrier in the home of the Gentile Cornelius. From that day to this, literally billions of people have heard what is by now, "the old, old story of Jesus and his love." Power. The power we affirm when we say, "I believe in the Holy Ghost."

Archbishop Temple called the Holy Spirit "the active energy of God." It is God at work in our lives, changing us. It was frightened disciples, huddled in fear behind closed doors, being transformed into confident evangelists, defying the power of Rome itself. It is you and me being changed, day by day, being enabled to love people we dislike, enabled to confront injustice at the cost of other people disliking us. The Holy Spirit brings power. "I believe in the Holy Ghost."

D. L. Moody was a shoe clerk who became a great evangelist for Jesus Christ. At one time, Moody visited a small church in Great Britain. When he got up to speak during the morning service, he faced the coldest, most apathetic congregation he had ever seen, and he was glad when the experience was over. He dreaded going back that evening, but unfortunately his presence had been advertised.

That evening service, though, was totally different. As he preached, Moody noticed some warmth in the crowd. Then there was more warmth. Finally, there was so much warmth that a revival broke out and, though Moody was engaged to be somewhere else the next day, he promised to come back in a few days and continue to preach, so that the promise of that wonderful evening could be fulfilled.

When he returned, Moody learned what had happened that unusual Sunday. An older woman in the congregation could no longer attend church but spent her days in a wheelchair. When she first read about D. L. Moody and his great gifts as an evangelist, she had prayed that he would one day come to visit her little church. Then when a relative came home from church that Sunday morning and told her the preacher had been D. L. Moody from America, she had prayed all afternoon, asking God to send the Spirit upon the congregation and fill it with a desire for repentance and new life in Christ.

According to Moody, what happened that remarkable evening was not his doing. It was the work of that woman in her wheelchair and of the powerful Spirit of God that had swept over the congregation, changing hearts and calling the entire church to new spiritual adventures.[1]

A bit scary, eh? As one commentator has said, "We all pray for the Holy Spirit, but as soon as the tongues of flame begin to appear we all run for the fire department."[2]

Still, we say "I believe in the Holy Ghost." Why? Because this is God at work in our world today, every minute of every hour of every day. It is good to know that when you need the divine presence in your life, God is not off on vacation somewhere. God is always present in the person of the Holy Spirit.

What will that mean in the nitty-gritty of life? After all, we have been insisting throughout this study that as we believe, so we behave. The abiding presence of the Spirit with us helps us behave.

Recall that passage from Galatians 5. The apostle Paul pictures human nature as possessing two sides. There is the flesh, which is our point of kinship with the animals and which is always pulling us down to our baser selves — "sexual immorality, impurity and debauchery; idolatry and witchcraft; hatred, discord, jealousy, fits of rage, selfish ambition, dissensions, factions and envy; drunkenness, orgies, and the like" (5:19-21). On the other side is our spirit, which is akin to God and which is always pulling us upward to our better selves. Paul pictures these two sides of human nature as in conflict, but he insists that it is possible for us, under the control of the Spirit, to be changed from our baser to our better selves. Call it being born again, call it regeneration, call it conversion, call it the new life of the Spirit, call it what you will; the claim of the Christian message is that we can be changed.

There is the fruit of the Spirit.[3] There is love and not just any old kind of love — *agape* love. It means unconquerable benevolence. It means that no matter what someone might do to us by way of insult or injury or humiliation we will never seek anything else but that person's highest good. It is a feeling of the mind as much as of the heart; it concerns the will as much as the emotions. It describes the deliberate effort — which we can make only with the help of God — never to seek anything but the best even for those who seek the worst for us.

There is joy — not the joy that comes from earthly things, still less from triumphing over someone else in competition. It is a joy whose foundation is God.

There is peace — not just the absence of conflict or freedom from trouble but everything that makes for a person's highest good. It means that tranquility of heart, which derives from the all-pervading consciousness that our times are in the hands of God.

There is patience and generally speaking the word is not used of patience in regard to things or events but in regard to people. It is the graciousness of the person who could exact revenge but does not, the person who is slow to anger. It is commonly used in the New Testament of the attitude of God toward you and me (Romans 2:4; Romans 9:22; 1 Timothy 1:16; 1 Peter 3:20).

There is goodness. It could also be translated kindness or even sweetness. It is a lovely word. Plutarch says that it has a far wider place than justice.

There is faithfulness — trustworthiness — it is the characteristic of the person who it reliable.

There is gentleness. In the New Testament, the word we translate here has three main meanings: 1) it means being submissive to the will of God; 2) it means being teachable, being not too proud to learn; and 3) most often of all, it means being considerate. Aristotle defined it as the midpoint between excessive anger and excessive angerlessness, the quality of the one who is always angry at the right time and never at the wrong time. This is the animal that has been tamed.

Finally, there is self-control. It is used of the athlete's discipline of the body and of the Christian's mastery of sex. Secular Greek uses the term in reference to the virtue of an emperor who never lets his private interests influence the government of his people. It is the virtue which makes you and me so much the masters of ourselves that we are fit to be servants of others.

"I believe in the Holy Ghost," and why not? If I can become all I ought to be, wonderful!

The good news of the gospel is that we *can* be changed. Wherever you look in the Bible you will find it. "If anyone is in Christ, he is a new creation; the old has gone, the new has come!" says Paul (2 Corinthians 5:17).

"No man need stay the way he is," says Harry Emerson Fosdick in one of his sermons to a generation past.

> *If I did not believe that human nature can be changed — the selfish man becoming unselfish, the drinking man becoming the sober man, the man who loses his temper becoming the man who controls his temper, the dishonest man becoming honorable, and the man of passion becoming the man of purity — then I would be forced to resign my job and go into some other business. I believe it can happen because I have seen it happen, and because I believe in the power of God which can make it happen.*[4]

Yes! Me, too. And that is why I can say with all my heart, "I believe in the Holy Ghost!" Can you?

1. John Killinger, *You are What You Believe: The Apostles' Creed for Today* (Nashville: Abingdon, 1990), pp. 87-88.

2. Melvin G. Kyle quoted by Addison Leitch, *Interpreting Basic Theology* (Great Neck, New York: Channel Press, 1961), p. 125.

3. The brief expositions that follow are from William Barclay, *The Daily Study Bible*, CD-ROM edition (Liguori, Missouri: Liguori Faithware, 1996). Used by permission of Westminster/John Knox Press.

4. Quoted by John A. Redhead Jr., *Uncommon Common Sense, Volume III, The Apostles' Creed* (Greensboro, North Carolina: Alexander McAlister Worth Foundation, 1997), pp. 157-158.

Questions For Reflection

1. Should the church update its terminology to fit modern understanding (such as "ghost" vs. "spirit") or retain the traditional language?

2. Many mainline Christians are uncomfortable with "Holy Ghost" talk. Why?

3. What are some of the gifts of the Holy Spirit that you have seen evidenced in your own Christian walk?

4. How have you experienced the guidance of the Holy Spirit in your life?

5. Can someone claim to be a Christian if they do not evidence the fruit of the Spirit?

Chapter 11

The Holy Catholic Church

We have stretched from the sublime, soaring through the heights of creation with almighty God; we have seen humanity at its best in the life and ministry of Jesus; we have seen a love that reaches down to the very depths of hell; we have joyously experienced resurrection, Christ's ascension to glory, and his commitment to work justice in this unjust world. We have been reminded of God's continuous action in our lives through the presence of the Holy Spirit. And now, "I believe in ... the holy catholic church...." We are tempted to say we have moved from the sublime to the ridiculous. Of all the affirmations we make in the Apostles' Creed, this one raises the most questions.

Let us take it one word at a time to see if we can make sense of it. "The holy catholic church" — *holy* — what do we mean when we call the church holy? The word "holy" literally means "separate" or "set apart." It is used to designate anything or anyone that belongs especially to God and thus is separated or set apart from the world. In the Bible, the priests of God are holy because they have to do with God. The temple is holy because it is a place set apart for the worship of God. The Bible is holy because it contains a revelation of God different from that which you will find in any other book. The church is holy because it is a fellowship with God and therefore is distinct from any other human association.

To modern minds, the word "holy" brings up a picture of something with a halo over its head — pious, pure, sinless. But that asks more of the word than is fair. If we need proof, all we have to do is say again, "I believe in the *holy* catholic church."

Is the church sinless? Of course not — the church is an association of sinners; in fact, that is the entrance requirement. In my Presbyterian tradition, the very first question we ask new members is, "Do you acknowledge yourself to be a sinner in the sight of God?" All of us can tell tales of ignorance and hypocrisy in the church — ministers who were deceitful, elders who were unbearable, men who were obstinate, and women who were silly and insufferable. This is part of the complaint against organized religion noted by some of our atheist detractors that we noted in the introduction to this volume.

Put all that together under one roof and the results are almost predictable. Crusades to recapture the holy land and free it from the "infidels"; Torquemada and the Spanish Inquisition; the persecution of the Reformers; the religious arguments in favor of slavery; and the silence of German Christians when Hitler persecuted the Jews or the Dutch Reformed church when South Africa instituted apartheid. "Frankly," wrote Leslie Weatherhead a half-century ago in his wonderfully insightful *The Christian Agnostic*, "I often wonder why so many people do go to church. Christianity must have a marvelous inherent power, or the churches would have killed it long ago."[1]

In spite of all that though, we continue to make our affirmation: "I believe in the holy, catholic church." Why? Precisely because the church is *holy* — set apart. For all its flaws and failures, the church belongs to God.

What about this word "catholic"? Lots of Protestants choke on this one because, when we hear the word, our mind jumps automatically to the church of Rome — pope, priests, nuns — the very church from which our forebears broke away hundreds of years ago. In fact, some Protestant congregations refuse to use the word "catholic" in their recitation of the creed — they offer substitutes: "I believe in the holy, Christian church" or "I believe in the holy, universal church." To be accurate, "universal" is the better substitute because that is what "catholic" really means. The earliest use of the word "catholic," as applied to the Christian church, is found in the writings of Ignatius in the early part of the second century. It meant "the whole body of believers, as distinguished from a group of Christians or an individual congregation."[2]

Some years ago, at a meeting of our Presbyterian General Assembly, a request was received from a presbytery asking for an explanatory statement on the word "catholic." The assembly answered by simply referring the presbytery to the Westminster

Confession of Faith which, at the time, was the primary doctrinal summary for Presbyterians in the USA:

> *The catholic or universal church, which is invisible, consists of the whole number of the elect, that have been, are, or shall be gathered into one, under Christ the head thereof ... The visible Church, which is also catholic or universal under the gospel (not confined to one nation as before under the law), consists of all those throughout the world that profess the true religion, together with their children; and is the Kingdom of the Lord Jesus Christ; the house and family of God ...* ("of the Church").

When the people of God was simply the Jewish nation, the church was not catholic. But with the expansion of the gospel, people of all nations, races, and languages were welcomed into the family of God. Suddenly, we had a catholic church. And ever since, our allegiance has been not to a racist church that accepts only one ethnic group, not to a national church limited by artificial boundaries, not to a denominational church that insists on a certain label, not even to a "one, true church" that denies the name of Christian to any who do not walk the walk and talk the talk in a certain specific way. Our allegiance has been to the church of Jesus Christ.

I read somewhere of a woman who was talking to her Presbyterian minister, taking him to task for injecting something into a worship service which, she said, was "not Presbyterian."

"Well," the minister replied, "you don't mean to say that you believe that the only way you can get to heaven is by being a Presbyterian, do you?"

She thought a minute and said, "No, not really. But no genteel person would think of going any other way."

Ha! "I believe in the holy *catholic* church." The word "catholic" is a good word, and it belongs to Presbyterians as much as it does to anyone else.

Finally, the word "church." What do we mean when we say "church"? Strange as it seems, nowhere in scripture do we find a definition of the word "church." We find a foundation for the church in our gospel lesson. Jesus asked the twelve, "Who do people say that the Son of Man is?" They responded with popular conjecture: John the Baptist, Elijah, Jeremiah, or some other of the ancient prophets. Then Jesus asked, "Who do you say that I am?" Simon Peter answers, "You are the Christ, the Son of the living God" (Matthew 16:13-16). This is the foundation of the church, this universally held belief that Jesus is the Christ, the Messiah, Jesus is Lord, and this is why Jesus would say, "... on this rock [this solid confessional foundation] I will build my church ..." (Matthew 16:18).

A foundation, but still no definition. Instead, we find descriptive pictures, metaphors, similes — students have found over ninety different descriptions of the church in the pages of the New Testament ... but no definition.

To define "church," some would refer to a specific building, some to a denomination. Some might use some of those New Testament phrases like "body of Christ" or "bride of Christ" or "servant." Most would probably insist on people being involved in any definition. For all the flaws that sinful people bring under steepled roofs and into stained-glass sanctuaries, there is no church without people.

As we say, scripture does not give us a definition of "church" but a little word study offers us a clue. Our word "church" comes from a Greek word *ekklesia*, which itself is made by combining two other words — *ek*, meaning "out," and *kaleo*, meaning "call." (And this is where the word "ecclesiastical" — meaning anything to do with church — comes from.) That would lead us to conclude that the church is those people whom God in Christ has *called out*.

"Called out?" For what? How about one simple sentence found in our *Presbyterian Study Catechism*? "The mission of the church is to bear witness to God's love for the world in Jesus Christ."[3] It's a simple sentence with a considerable challenge.

For all its flaws, the church has done a mighty work. This called-out church has given the world ideals ... ideals like religious and political liberty ... ideals like racial unity, social justice, and human brotherhood. Through the work of the church and the convictions that have come from her, the most sinful of the world's economic and social and political evils have been driven to defeat or shamed into hiding. Who led the battle against human slavery in this nation in the last century? Who has been in the forefront of America's quest for racial equality? Who has been most vocal in its concern for peace among nations? The church and her people have been the conscience of the world.

The called-out church has provided bold messengers ... the first pioneers and adventurers into the dark and neglected areas of the earth — the William Careys, the David Brainards, the Hudson Taylors, the David Livingstons — not simply for the sake of pushing beyond frontiers but that the people who live there might come to know the fullness of God's blessing in Jesus Christ. The messengers of the church have always taken the lead in the civilizing and enlightening work of the world.

The messengers of the called-out church, not medical people as such, have been the first to go into all parts of the earth with the science of sanitation, nutrition, and physical healing. How many hospitals are named "Baptist" or "Methodist" or "Presbyterian"?

Not professional educators but the messengers of the called-out church have reduced languages to writing, established schools, and set up printing presses for the distribution of the word of God. The first Sunday schools were established, not simply to teach Bible stories to youngsters, but to offer what was then the only opportunity for them to learn to read and write. Public education in America grew out of the selfless work of the church.

Not social reformers but the messengers of the called-out church have taken the lead in the fight against poverty, famine, and plague. The church has elevated the status of women, created new conditions for childhood, established orphanages, day care centers, asylums, homes for the aged, and others who need help.

History offers no parallel to the unselfish and uplifting work of the called-out church. There is no question that what goes on in parliaments and congresses, in council halls and chambers of commerce, and in the highest courts of the nations is always of importance to humanity. But when the world is out of joint, when people's minds are disordered and their hearts are failing them for fear, then the thing of supreme importance is the living church, with all of her sanctuaries of worship and her avenues of service, where men and women come to have their faith strengthened, their thoughts clarified, their ideas uplifted, their convictions born, and their characters created. The called-out church, for all her faults, is the institution of supreme significance and value in the world through the ages.

Remember the words of the catechism: "The mission of the church is to bear witness to God's love for the world in Jesus Christ." It's a simple sentence with a considerable challenge. For all the good works the church has offered, those pale by comparison to the one thing that the church uniquely did and continues to do — it has introduced the world to Jesus Christ. It was the called-out church that preserved those magnificent words, "For God so loved the world that he gave his only begotten Son." It was the called-out church that taught us, "Believe in the Lord Jesus Christ and you shall be saved." We know Christ because the called-out church brought us to him. The called-out church gave us a right start, and the called-out church *tries* to keep us on the right road.

I read somewhere that near a church in Kansas there can be seen in a cement sidewalk the prints of two baby feet pointing toward the building. It was said that some years ago, when the sidewalk was being laid, a mother secured permission to stand her baby boy on the wet cement. The mother had wanted to start her son in the right direction. She pointed him to the church.

"I believe in the holy catholic church." Jack Redhead tells of a Chinese proverb to the effect that there are five points to the compass: north, east, south, west, and the point where you are. The holy catholic church is scattered to the four points of the compass, but we come back eventually to the point where we are because our attitude toward the universal church is revealed in our attitude toward the local church.[4] Remember, as we believe, so we behave. Where are you today? In a society for which church is optional and there are wonderful excuses to ignore it, the choice is yours. As for me, "I believe in the holy catholic church."

1. Leslie Weatherhead, *The Christian Agnostic* (New York, Abingdon Press, 1965).

2. John A. Redhead Jr., *Uncommon Common Sense, Volume III: The Apostles' Creed* (Greensboro, North Carolina: Worth Family Foundation, 1997), p. 168.

3. Q. 63, *Presbyterian Study Catechism*, approved by the 210th General Assembly (1998).

4. *Op cit*, Redhead, p. 172.

Questions For Reflection

1. What is wrong with the church?

2. What is right with the church?

3. With all the denominational divisions, how can we continue to talk about *one* church of Jesus Christ?

4. What is the primary task of the church?

5. When you invite someone to your church, what do you say?

Chapter 12

The Communion Of Saints

"I believe in the Holy Ghost, the holy catholic church, the communion of Saints...." Those last two are so intertwined that they are often considered together.

Both are wonderful affirmations, but *do* have negative connotations. Just as we noted in the preceding chapter that the "holy catholic church" often looks very *un*holy, the "communion of saints" is often not very saintly.

There is an ancient tale of a young rabbi who found a serious problem in his new congregation. During the Friday service, half the congregation stood for the prayers and half remained seated, and each side shouted at the other, insisting that theirs was the true tradition. Nothing the rabbi said or did moved toward solving the impasse. Finally, in desperation, the young rabbi sought out the synagogue's 99-year-old founder. He met the old rabbi in the nursing home and poured out his troubles. "So tell me," he pleaded, "was it the tradition for the congregation to stand during the prayers?"

"No," answered the old rabbi.

"Ah," responded the younger man, "then it was the tradition to sit during the prayers."

"No," answered the old rabbi.

"Well," the young rabbi responded, "what we have is complete chaos! Half the people stand and shout, and the other half sit and scream."

"Ah," said the old man, "that was the tradition."

Sound familiar? I hate to imagine how many congregations that could describe. Years ago, I briefly served a church where the officers were divided into what may as well have been two armed camps — the deacons versus the elders. For what seemed like generations these two groups had squabbled about anything and everything. Pastors would accept the call to that pulpit, arrive in town, quickly see the problem, then get in between the two groups to try to make peace. Pity the poor pastor. Like the fellow who did not want to take sides in the War between the States and advertised his neutrality by wearing a blue coat and gray pants — the rebels shot him in the coat and the yankees shot him in the pants! The pastors would get it from both sides and the result in that congregation was, in 140 years of history, they had gone through 35 preachers, 29 of whom lasted three years or less. Sing it children: "And they'll know we are Christians by our love, by our love, and they'll know we are Christians by our love." Ah, yes, the communion of saints, indeed!

A word here about our terms. Communion — if asked about it, what would jump to most people's minds first is the Lord's Supper. That is fine, as far as it goes. However, for the purpose of our affirmation we should understand communion, as one commentator suggests, as *fellowship-plus*. "It is more than the good time that people have when kindred spirits get together. It is rather the comradeship of those who know and enjoy the knowledge that they share the same heritage, the same values, and the same destiny."[1]

What do we in the church share? Sainthood ... at least in the biblical sense, if not the popular. If you asked most folks what a saint is, you might get definitions like "someone who is particularly good or godly," or perhaps "some special person who has been designated for veneration by the church." Biblically, we in the church are *all* saints — the word comes from the same root as our word "holy," which we have learned previously does not mean pious or pure but rather "set apart." Look at the apostle Paul's writings; the salutations on his letters say, "To all God's beloved in Rome, who are called to be saints," or "To the church of God which is at Corinth ... called to be saints...." or "To all the saints in Christ Jesus who are at Philippi...." Saints every one — were these folks particularly pious or pure? Of course not — no more than we are. But the designation stands. We in the church are set apart — "saints" — because of our relationship with Jesus Christ, even though there are times when our behavior is not very saintly.

Would you like some help in that regard? Paul has some wonderful suggestions in Romans 12:

*Therefore, I urge you, brothers [and sisters], in view of
God's mercy, to offer your bodies as living sacrifices,
holy and pleasing to God — this is your spiritual act of
worship. Do not conform any longer to the pattern of
this world, but be transformed by the renewing of your
mind. Then you will be able to test and approve what
God's will is — his good, pleasing and perfect will.*
— Romans 12:1-2

Start by remembering who you are and *whose* you are. If we
saints are God's people, our day-to-day activities — the office, the
factory, the school, the store — become offerings. God's priorities
become our priorities.

Paul continues: "... I say to every one of you: Do not think of
yourself more highly than you ought, but rather think of yourself
with sober judgment, in accordance with the measure of faith God
has given you" (v. 3). Good advice, particularly to church folks
who sometimes think they have a corner on "the truth."

Paul goes on to describe our work together and uses that metaphor he enjoys so much describing the church as a *body*. Just as
different parts of the human body have different tasks, the same is
true in the church. Paul says take a look at what task you are suited
for, then do it.

"Love must be sincere ..." (v. 9) — *agape* love, the love that is
only interested in the welfare of the beloved, no matter what. "Hate
what is evil, cling to what is good ..." — no compromises with sin.

This one is special: "Be devoted to one another in brotherly
love. Honor one another above yourselves" (v. 10). What a wonderful church it is when that is the rule of behavior — genuine
caring and genuine gratitude.

"Never be lacking in zeal, but keep your spiritual fervor, serv-
ing the Lord" (v. 11). The venerable William Barclay wrote:

*There is a certain intensity in the Christian life; there
is no room for lethargy in it. The Christian cannot take
things in an easy-going way, for the world is always a
battleground between good and evil, the time is short,*

and life is a preparation for eternity. The Christian may
burn out, but [the Christian] must not rust out.[2]

Paul's list continues: "Be joyful in hope, patient in affliction ..." (v. 12). We do have hope and we can be patient when things are awful, because way, way down, in the very depths of our being, we know how the story ends, and we know who wins. "Faithful in prayer" (v. 12) — prayer is the oil that makes the machinery of life work. "Share with God's people who are in need. Practice hospitality" (v. 13). Have open hearts and open hands. God's people are generous people. "Bless those who persecute you; bless and do not curse" (v. 14). The same instruction Jesus gave concerning the way to deal with enemies.

Here is one that is incredibly important. "Rejoice with those who rejoice, mourn with those who mourn" (v. 15). Who of those in our lives mean the most to us? Those who are truly happy at our successes, whose words of congratulation are genuine. Those who, in times of hurt, instead of giving solutions or cures, choose rather to share our pain and touch our wounds with a warm and tender hand. The one who can be silent with us in a moment of despair, who can stay with us in an hour of grief, who does not try to force-feed us some cure, who is content to simply *be* there, that one is truly a friend.

Paul's advice continues: "Live in harmony with one another." That makes sense. Churches that are out of harmony rarely accomplish much. "Do not be proud, but be willing to associate with people of low position. Do not be conceited" (v. 16). An emphasis on perspective again. Get your nose out of the air. And remember, conceit is ugly. "Do not repay anyone evil for evil." Or, more clearly, "Be careful to do what is right in the eyes of everybody" (v. 17). Your behavior must not only *be* good, it should *look* good as well, and especially to those on the outside looking in.

One more bit of apostolic advice: "If it is possible, as far as it depends on you, live at peace with everyone" (v. 18). What can we say other than "Amen and amen"? Any congregation that can pattern itself after such a model is one I would be proud to be a part of. "I believe in the communion of saints."

In John Killinger's wonderful little book on the Apostles' Creed, he writes,

> *I used to wonder why the creed does not say anything about love. Love is so important in the Christian's life. Paul described it in his letter to the Corinthians as the crowning glory of our existence, the single quality that outranks and outlasts all others. Yet the creed is mysteriously silent about it. Then one day I was praying and thinking about the saints in heaven — especially my mother — who were praying for me, and I realized, "Love is there! It is in the community of saints! That's what the communion of saints is all about! It's why Jesus, at the last supper, talked about abiding in him and loving one another at the same time. They belong together — being in him and loving." That's the real meaning of the communion of saints, and most of the time we forget it and neglect to draw our strength from it.*[3]

Too bad.

"I believe in the communion of saints." We continue to insist, as we believe, so we behave. Lila Craig believes. You can tell. A Nashville newspaper carried a tongue-in-cheek story about Lila who at the time of the story had not missed attending church in 1,040 Sundays although she was in her eighties. The editor commented:

> *It makes one wonder, what's the matter with Mrs. Craig? Doesn't it ever rain or snow in her town on Sunday? Doesn't she ever have unexpected company? How is it that she never goes anywhere on Saturday night so that she's too tired to attend the worship service the next morning? Doesn't she ever "beg off" to attend picnics or family reunions, or have headaches, colds, nervous spells, or tired feelings? Doesn't she ever oversleep or need time to read her Sunday newspaper? Hasn't she ever become angry at the minister or had her feelings hurt by someone and felt justified in staying home to*

hear a good sermon on the radio or TV? What's the
matter with Mrs. Craig anyway?[4]

I will tell you what the matter is — she believes in the communion of saints.

There is a wonderful passage near the end of the book of Hebrews that many know fondly as "Faith's Hall of Fame." The writer offers a long list of great men and women of God from the days of pre-history on down. Famous names like Abraham, Isaac, Jacob, and Moses, plus some others not so famous but equally important, such as Rahab, Barak, Samson, Jephthah, and on and on and on. Why such a list? The author offers them as an encouragement to us in our own faith journey. They are called a "great cloud of witnesses" (Romans 12:1). We cannot say positively if the writer intends to convey that these faithful men and women who have gone before actually see us and cheer us on as we run our own daily race, or whether the word "witness" is simply to be understood as one who has proclaimed God's truth to the world, just as when we speak of a witness on the stand in a court of law. We do not know. If the word does not say specifically that those faithful folk *can* see us, it does not say that they *cannot*, either. What a thought! That we run our race in front of all history and heaven.

Yonder they are. There is the gallery of the prophets: Samuel, Isaiah, and Jeremiah. Over there, the gallery of the apostles: Peter, James, John, and Paul. There are the reformers: Luther, Calvin, and Knox. Over there is the gallery of the great evangelists: Wesley, Whitefield, and Spurgeon. There are the missionaries: David Brainard, Hudson Taylor, and David Livingstone. And over here, a gallery that perhaps means more to you and me than all the others, the one where sit our own fathers and mothers, brothers and sisters, dear friends whose own race is now done, those who gave us a solid foundation for our beliefs and a solid footing for our faith. They are the witnesses who surround us, watching our conflicts and rejoicing in our victories. Above them, and watching with them, the one who died that they and we might live, our Lord and Savior, Jesus Christ. "I believe in the communion of saints."

Years ago, I read of a little boy who was asked if he knew what a saint was. The lad thought for a moment, remembered the stained-glass windows in his church and replied, "The saints are the ones the light shines through." Truer words were never spoken.

"Lord, I want to be in that number."

---

1. B. Clayton Bell, *Moorings in a World Adrift: Answers for Christians Who Dare to Ask Why* (San Francisco: HarperSanFrancisco, 1990), p. 92.

2. William Barclay, *The Daily Study Bible*, CD-ROM edition (Liguori, Missouri: Liguori Faithware, 1996). Used by permission of Westminster/John Knox Press.

3. John Killinger, *You are What You Believe: The Apostles' Creed for Today* (Nashville: Abingdon, 1990), p. 103.

4. Paul Kabo, via Ecunet, "Sermonshop Sermons," #1379.

Questions For Reflection

1. When you think of a "saint" who is it? Why?

2. What are some ways that your church encourages the "communion of the saints"?

3. What do you think of Lila Craig's record of church attendance? Should that kind of commitment be the norm or the exception?

4. If you knew that the saints who have passed on could see you as you run your life's race, what one person would you want watching? Why?

5. In what ways would you want people to say the "light shines through" you?

Chapter 13

The Forgiveness Of Sins

"I believe in the Holy Ghost, the holy catholic church, the communion of saints, the forgiveness of sins...."

Martin Luther called this the most important affirmation in the entire creed. He said, "If that is not true, what does it matter whether God is almighty or that Jesus Christ was born and died and rose again? It is because these things have a bearing on my forgiveness that they are important to me."

"I believe in the forgiveness of sins." Sadly, there is not a lot of forgiveness out there these days. Parents cannot forgive rebellious children and therefore abuse them; children cannot forgive imperfect parents and therefore neglect them; students cannot forgive insults so they shoot up the school; Sunnis cannot forgive Shias, and neither can they forgive America.

Two little brothers, Harry and James, had finished supper and were playing until bedtime. Somehow, Harry hit James with a stick, and tears and bitter words followed. Charges and accusations were still being exchanged as mother prepared them for bed. The mother instructed, "Now James, before you go to bed you're going to have to forgive your brother."

James was thoughtful for a few moments, and then he replied, "Well, okay, I'll forgive him tonight, but if I don't die before then, he'd better look out in the morning."[1]

"I believe in the forgiveness of sins." Whose forgiveness? First and foremost, *God's* forgiveness. The ancients counted on it. Listen again to the psalmist:

> *Bless the Lord, O my soul, and all that is within me, bless his holy name. Bless the Lord, O my soul, and do not forget all his benefits — who forgives all your iniquity ... He does not deal with us according to our sins, nor repay us according to our iniquities. For as the heavens are high above the earth, so great is his steadfast love toward those who fear him; as far as the east*

is from the west, so far he removes our transgressions
from us.   — Psalm 103:1-3a, 10-12 (NRSV)

From the pages of the Old Testament on into the gospels and the story of Jesus and the cross, the love and forgiveness of God are writ large. Luther understood it ... finally. You and I do too ... sometimes. My eminently quotable friend and colleague, Carlos Wilton, writes:

> *Ours is a self-confident, even self-promoting, age. Many people you or I are likely to encounter will tell us they've had it with guilt; that they don't want to hear any more about sin; that they believe every person's got lots of good within them — deep down, all you've got to do is help them "realize their potential." But I'm convinced it's all a front, a facade, a masquerade. Guilt is alive and well; you can't kill it that easily.*[2]

There is a true story of a Catholic priest living in the Philippines, a much-beloved man of God who once carried a secret burden of long-past sin buried deep in his heart. He had committed that sin once, many years before, during his time in seminary. No one else knew of this sin. He had repented of it but had suffered years of remorse for it. He had felt no peace, no inner joy, and no sense of God's forgiveness.

There was a woman in this priest's parish who deeply loved God, and who claimed to have visions in which she spoke with Christ, and he with her. As might be expected, the priest was skeptical of her claims, so to test her visions he said to her, "You say you actually speak with Christ in your visions. Let me ask you a favor. The next time you have one of these visions, I want you to ask him what sin your priest committed while he was in seminary."

The woman agreed and went home. When she returned to the church a few days later, the priest asked, "Well, did Christ visit you in your dreams?"

"Yes, he did," she replied.

"And did you ask him what sin I committed in seminary?"

"Yes, I asked him."

116

"Well, what did he say?"

"He said, 'I don't remember.' "[3]

"... as far as the east is from the west, so far he removes our transgressions from us." "I believe in the forgiveness of sins."

This forgiveness in which we say we believe is not limited to God, though. Forgiveness is part and parcel of human life. In fact, in the Lord's Prayer, we affirm the necessity of a forgiving spirit to even begin to experience the forgiveness of God. "Forgive us our debts ... our trespasses, our sins ... as we forgive those who sin against us." Throughout our study of the Creed, we have been insisting that as we believe, so we behave. Nowhere is that any more evident than in this issue of forgiveness.

In the late '90s, after the impeachment trial of President Clinton was finally over, the president spoke briefly on the White House lawn. There was no gloating at the fact that neither of the two articles had come close to passing, just the suggestion that it was time for him, for the congress, for the country, to move on. He turned away from the podium after his remarks and began walking back to the oval office without taking any questions from reporters. But ABC's irrepressible Sam Donaldson asked loudly, "In your heart, sir, can you forgive and forget?"

The president paused, turned around, and came back to the microphone. He said, "I believe any person who asks for forgiveness has to be prepared to give it."

A few years ago, Presbyterian minister, Michael Lindvall, wrote a delightful little book comprised of vignettes from the life of a small-town pastor called *The Good News From North Haven*. One of the stories has to do with the pastor's visit to the barbershop. During the course of their conversation, the barber tells the minister how his father used to come home every Saturday night as drunk as a skunk and beat the tar out of him and his mother. The pastor's response was to look at the man in the mirror, put his hands on the hands that were resting on his shoulders and say, "Just because you forgive someone doesn't mean that what they did to you was right."[4] That needs to be said.

Could you use some guidance on *how* to forgive? Many of us get caught so deeply in the web of resentments that we cannot pick our way out of it. Here are some points from the literature of one of the twelve-step programs:

> *Many of us have been told all our lives that we ought to forgive those who wrong us, but rarely have we been taught how to do so.*

1. *Write down in black and white the reasons why we are angry with (someone). Writing clarifies emotions which have been confused and buried in us, sometimes for years. Also by setting down our grievances in black and white, we place a boundary around them. Our grievances are only so big and no bigger. The hurt had a beginning and it can have an end.*

2. *Consider "giving away" (telling) what we have written to some trusted person. Consider symbolically releasing the hurt, such as by burning or tearing up the paper.*

3. *Pray.*
   a. *Pray for willingness to forgive.*
   b. *Pray for the person who has wronged us, daily, asking God to bless them with good things we want for ourselves. If we keep praying for them faithfully, sooner or later our feelings will change. When our feelings change, when we find ourselves being sincere in asking God to bless our former enemies, then we will know we have forgiven them.*

Remember, it is possible to be *willing* to do something we do not *want* to do.

As Lewis Smedes has written, "To forgive is to put down your fifty-pound pack after a ten-mile climb up a mountain. To forgive is to fall into a chair after running a marathon. To forgive is to set a prisoner free and discover that prisoner is you. To forgive is to reach back into your hurting past and recreate it in your memory so that you can begin again."[5] Do you need to forgive someone?

An oft-repeated story comes from a little village in Spain. Father and son argue and say things they should never have said. The son, a boy named Paco, runs away to the big city of Madrid. Weeks go by, then months, and the father comes to regret his anger. He rehearses, over and over again in his mind, the apology he will offer to his son when he returns. Yet, Paco does not come back. The father begins to fear he has lost his son forever. Finally, the father devises a plan. He travels to the city, armed with posters that he puts up on every wall and tree. He takes out a classified ad in the newspaper. Everywhere the message is the same:

> Dear Paco,
> Meet me in front of the newspaper office tomorrow at noon. All is forgiven. I love you.
> Your father

Now, "Paco" is a very common name in Spain — like "John" or "Jim" in the US. Remember, too, that the father did not sign his posters, or his classified ad, with anything except "Your father."

By twelve o'clock the next day, as the story goes, Paco is waiting outside the newspaper building; he and his father have a joyful reunion. Yet along with the son, there are 800 other men named Paco, gathered there, every last one of them hoping it was his father who took out the ad and nailed up the posters.

"I believe in the forgiveness of sins."

Do you believe? Again, as we believe, so we behave. In fact, according to the apostle Paul, not only so we behave, so we preach. In 2 Corinthians we find, "God was reconciling the world to himself in Christ, not counting men's sins against them. And he has committed to us the message of reconciliation. We are therefore Christ's ambassadors, as though God were making his appeal through us" (5:19-20).

Christ's *ambassadors*! That is a high calling indeed. Not many more responsible positions than this. An ambassador speaks on behalf of his or her own country or sovereign. When a US ambassador speaks, his or her voice is the voice of the United States. An ambassador for Christ is the voice that brings the message of Jesus to the human situation. The honor of a country is in its ambassador's hands. The country represented is judged by the ambassador. Words are heard, deeds are seen, and people say, "That is the way the country speaks and acts." Here is our proud privilege and almost terrifying task. The honor of Christ and of the church are in our hands.

As ambassadors our message from our sovereign is forgiveness. No need for the church to offer moral exhortations that would come better at a Rotary or Lions' Club luncheon. We can cut down on offering social judgments that are better given at political conventions. We can modify our efforts at personal therapy that are better handled by psychiatrists and psychologists. We have a word that the world is desperate to hear, a word that no one else can offer — forgiveness.

Forgiveness is power ... the power to be renewed and to renew ... the power to be cleansed and to clean. Forgiveness is the power to be restored and to restore to favor and wholeness. That is what Luther came to understand, and that is our message as ambassadors for Christ. Nothing else can rebuild our relationship with God the way forgiveness can. Nothing else can so change an individual the way forgiveness can. Nothing else can change international relations the way forgiveness can. Power. It may be the most positive power in all the world.

No wonder we make our affirmation. Over and over we say it, then over and over and over again. "I believe in the forgiveness of sins."

---

1. James S. Hewett, *Illustrations Unlimited* (Wheaton, Illinois: Tyndale House Publishers, Inc., 1988), p. 223.

2. Carlos Wilton, "Of Fire and Forgiveness," unpublished sermon delivered at Point Pleasant Presbyterian Church, Point Pleasant, New Jersey, June 16, 1996.

3. Bruce Larson in Robert Lee Davis' *A Forgiving God in an Unforgiving World* (Eugene, Oregon: Harvest House Publishers, 1984).

4. Michael Lindvall, *The Good News From North Haven* (New York: Pocket Books, 1992).

5. Lewis Smedes, "Forgiveness: The Power to Change the Past," *Christianity Today*, 1/7/83, p. 26.

Questions For Reflection

1. Forgiveness has been called the power to change the past. Is that true? Why or why not?

2. We often hear "forgive and forget." Is that advisable? Is it possible?

3. We also hear, "Don't get mad, get even." How does that square with the prayer we make to "forgive us our sins as we forgive those who sin against us"?

4. In your own experience have you ever been unexpectedly forgiven of something? How did you react?

5. Is there someone you need to forgive right now?

Chapter 14

The Resurrection Of The Body

"I believe in the Holy Ghost, the holy catholic church, the communion of saints, the forgiveness of sins, the resurrection of the body...."

As I began to ponder this affirmation, I asked my dear wife what I could say that would be new and exciting and interesting about "I believe in the resurrection of the body." Her response: "I have no idea; it has never been a burning issue with me." What's that you say? Amen? True enough, this is not a subject upon which we dwell too much. Except in the face of death, we almost never consider it. But when confronted with issues of mortality ... our own or that of those we love ... we become interested.

"I believe in the resurrection of the body." The affirmation is virtually impossible to explain. The best minds in the church have labored for nearly twenty centuries to do so. The language itself is a problem. After all, we know that, following death, our bodies deteriorate: "Earth to earth, ashes to ashes, dust to dust," as our funeral services say. The most secure burial vault in the world will not prevent the process. We remember the little boy who looks under his bed, sees the dust bunnies, remembers the dust-to-dust language, and yells to Mom, "Come quick and check under this bed. If I'm not mistaken, we got somebody here either comin' or goin'."

Perhaps that is one of the reasons so many folks, when thinking about what life lies beyond this one, use phrases like the "immortality of the soul" rather than "resurrection of the body." Indeed, nowhere in scripture is it said that the soul will survive death in some inevitable and automatic fashion, as though the soul were ultimately independent of the body and had some kind of inherent immortality. That is a Greek idea. Greek philosophers described the soul as a little spark of the divine temporarily imprisoned within a material body (which is inherently evil). The body — the prison house — is of this world and will die, but the spirit, the spark, is immortal and is released from the "prison house" upon death. It is this spiritual part of us human beings that will survive death. So said the Greeks. But the Hebrews saw the issue quite differently. A human being is not easily separable into body and soul, but is an integrated, indivisible unit, everything combining to make a person. If there is to be a future life, then somehow God has to re-create the whole person after death, not just this or that part. Understand this: In Christian teaching, eternal life is not due to some property intrinsic to the soul; it is entirely a gift of God.

So saying, the church continues to use the "immortal soul" language without batting a theological eye. As Al Winn suggests, the picture of it is clear in our minds: The body is the cocoon, the soul is the butterfly. The soul flutters away in the sunlight, and no one has any further regard for the dry, decaying, discarded cocoon.[1] Then we are jolted by this weekly affirmation concerning belief in the resurrection of the body.

We do have a bit of a love-hate relationship with our bodies, don't we? On the one hand, we try to take care of them. We wash them, shave them, primp them, paint them, nourish them, exercise them, occasionally indulge them, and do all in our power to ease their pains. On the other hand, the result of all that effort is rarely satisfactory: too big, too little, bad hair, no hair, and, as time goes on, everything just sags.

Two elderly residents of a nursing home were sitting in the lounge when suddenly a sweet old lady wandered out of her room and down the hall without any clothes. One said to the other, "Did you see that?" The second responded, "Yeah, but whatever she was wearing sure needed ironing."

Be honest — do you really want this body, this old cocoon, resurrected? Not me. There is too much about this one that is *wrong*! First and foremost, there is too much of it. All my life I have had to fight the battle of the bulge, and I am tired of it. My resurrection body will be skinny; after all, scripture says there will be no more tears in heaven, and if I am not skinny, I will cry! Then there are the ears that do not hear properly, eyes that need glasses, the nose that gets clogged during allergy seasons, the blood pressure that wants to make medical history, and, in general, a mind that writes checks that the body cannot cash. Sound familiar? Is this what we want to rise again? Get real!

Week in and week out we say, "I believe in the resurrection of the body." Why? Simple. This is what the Bible teaches.

Check out 1 Corinthians, chapter 15. Questions had been raised in the church in Corinth concerning a Christian understanding of life after death. For the apostle Paul, it came down to one word: resurrection. First, there was the resurrection of Jesus. Then there will be resurrection for us all. What will that entail, these Corinthians ask. After all, they had heard the stories about Jesus' bodily resurrection from the tomb, but their Greek heritage had trained them to discount the body (the "prison house") as evil and something to be gratefully discarded. Resurrection of the body? What kind of body will this be?

This is no foolish question. There are oodles of possibilities. What about the fourteen-year-old girl killed in an automobile accident; will she be perpetually fourteen? Or the lady who succumbed to a long battle with cancer at age 68; will she be 68? What about those who die in infancy or what about aborted fetuses? How about those who have lost arms or legs in accidents? What about the thalidomide babies born with seal flippers? Will we still be male and female with all the appropriate equipment? People have been amused for a good many years (in a gruesome sort of way) by a newspaper account some years ago with the heading, "Who Ate Roger Williams' Bones?" A historical society set out to dig up Roger Williams' bones and bury them in a better place only to discover that an apple tree had grown on his original burial plot, and much of Roger Williams had ended up in apples, and the apples had ended up in a lot of other people.[2] What about old Roger?

The apostle Paul answers with an analogy: a seed. The seed is put in the ground and "dies," but in due time it rises again; and does so with a very different kind of body from that with which it was sown. What that says is what we shall be on the other side is somehow contained in who we are on this side, but writ very large. Just as the apple tree comes from the apple seed and the peach tree from the peach seed — from the very seed that dies, not from some seed-in-general — so we shall come from the body-mind

125

combination we are now, but far more than anyone could tell by looking at us now.

Speaking of looking at us, the question of recognizability arises. If we go through such an amazing metamorphosis as seed to tree, will anyone be able to tell who we are? Absolutely. What has been our experience up to this point? In our lives, we have gone through major bodily changes — infancy, childhood, adulthood, and beyond. Science tells us that our bodies go through a 100% cellular change every seven years — that means if you are 35, you have already gone through five brand new bodies. But you are still *you*, and your friends and family know you as you — amazing.

On a deeper level, the answer to the recognizability question must be absolute! Recognizability is the key to our identity. For example, if I suddenly, in a fit of insanity, chose to throw over my life and all that is in it, head off to a new part of the country to establish a new life and a new name, nothing could stop me *unless* someone recognized me. Our identity, for good or ill, is inextricably tied to being recognized. If, right at this moment, no one recognized David Leininger, I may as well be Joe Blow. If, when I get to the other side, and this fat seed becomes a skinny tree, but no one recognizes me, I'll be Joe Blow all over again. We *will* know one another or else resurrection is not worth the bother.

"I believe in the resurrection of the body." Yes, the body will be different. Paul says, "The body that is sown is perishable, it is raised imperishable" (1 Corinthians 15:42). He knew just as we all do that these earthly bodies of ours deteriorate. On the other side, what a change! Musicians won't go deaf; artists won't go blind; singers won't lose their voices. No more of the physical limitations that keep us from being all that we can be.

Paul says the change involves more than just physical characteristics. He says, "It is sown in dishonor, it is raised in glory" (1 Corinthians 15:43a). For many of us, some of the saddest pages in the history of our lives came because passions got out of hand. We read about the epidemic of AIDS, the madness of child abuse, the insanity of drunken drivers murdering people on the highway. Yes, we dishonor the bodies we have, but our resurrection bodies will have passions we can control. What a blessing that will be!

Paul says the blessings will not stop even there: "It is sown in weakness, it is raised in power" (1 Corinthians 15:43b). Have you ever felt limited by the body you have? Of course! And the older we get, the more frequently we feel it. Nothing to be ashamed of — it is a fact of life. Quite frankly, many of God's creatures have far more ounce-for-ounce capability than we humans do. The lowly little ant has a life span of all of eight or ten weeks and then passes on into oblivion. Even that insignificant little ant is able to carry burdens that are nineteen times heavier than itself. Can we do that? Not without a truck! Will we be able to do that with our new resurrection bodies? Who knows? Paul does not give us the details. We can be sure that our capacities will be significantly improved.

Then there is one more thing: Paul says, "It is sown a natural (or physical) body, it is raised a spiritual body" (1 Corinthians 15:44). That does not mean we will be Casper the Friendly Ghost. We will have a body! But it is going to be different from what we are used to. The simplest way to explain it is to say that our capacity for spiritual things will be enhanced. For those who struggle to worship for even an hour a week, one would certainly hope.

There is one other aspect of the resurrection life that is important to us, which Paul does not discuss in this chapter ... family reunion. Paul did not discuss it, but Jesus did.

If you recall, some folks who did not believe in life after death confronted Jesus one day with a strange scenario (Matthew 22:23-28). They described a childless woman whose husband died. Tradition demanded that her husband's brother marry her, which he did — then *he* died. The next brother married her and *he* died. This first-century Typhoid Mary went through seven brothers before she finally ran out (and I tell you, had I been number six or seven, I would have run out). The question posed to Jesus was, "In the afterlife, whose wife will she be?" Jesus responded, "Don't worry about that. Family relationships are going to be different over there."

Oh, really? Frankly, the idea of an afterlife for me without my wife and children would be hell, not heaven. But if we think about it without emotion getting in the way, we realize that if God says earthly relationships will be changed, the change will be for the better. If God has not chosen to explain just how the changes will be made, perhaps it is because we would not understand the explanation anyway.

My children are grown. David likes women, Erin likes men. This is a bit of a change for them, because I can recall a time not many years ago that neither one cared very much for the opposite sex. I could have told them back then that things would change, but it would not have mattered. I could have explained to them the incredible joy of married love as they will eventually experience it, but what good would that have done? They would not have understood. Only when they began to mature were they able to appreciate anything I might say on that subject. That analogy may explain why God has not chosen to let us in on what kind of relationships are in store for us in heaven. We would not understand anyway.

Again, Paul says:

> When the perishable has been clothed with the imperishable, and the mortal with immortality, then the saying that is written will come true: "Death has been swallowed up in victory ... Where, O death, is your victory? Where, O death, is your sting?" The sting of death is sin, and the power of sin is the law. But thanks be to God! He gives us the victory through our Lord Jesus Christ.   — 1 Corinthians 15:54-57

"I believe in the resurrection of the body!" Remember, as we believe, so we behave. "Therefore, my dear brothers (and sisters)," Paul says, "Let nothing move you. Always give yourselves fully to the work of the Lord, because you know that your labor in the Lord is not in vain." Yes!

"I believe in the resurrection of the body." Not just *any* body, either. In the richly descriptive words of John Killinger, "It will be glorious, like the 'Hallelujah Chorus' in the flesh, embodied in a person. Like the sun breaking over the Rocky Mountains in the early morning or settling its colorful petticoats along the Pacific shore at twilight. Like a thousand mockingbirds all whistling and yodeling and singing in unison, or a flock of a million flamingos all taking flight at once!"[3] That will be glory!

Yes, I believe. "I believe in the resurrection of the body."

---

1. Albert Curry Winn, *A Christian Primer: The Prayer, The Creed, The Commandments* (Louisville: Westminster/John Knox Press, 1990), p. 176.

2. Addison Leitch, *A Layman's Guide to Presbyterian Beliefs* (Grand Rapids, Michigan: Zondervan Publishing, 1967), p. 133.

3. John Killinger, *You Are What You Believe: The Apostles' Creed for Today* (Nashville: Abingdon, 1990), p. 115.

Questions For Reflection

1. If the issue of "the resurrection of the body" was never a burning issue for the author's wife, has it ever been for you? Why or why not?

2. What will your resurrection body look like?

3. What would you like to be able to do with your new body that you are not able to do now?

4. What would your life be like if no one were able to recognize you?

5. If family relationships are to be different (and we trust better) in the resurrection, what differences would you like to see?

Chapter 15

The Life Everlasting

For God so loved the world, that he gave his only begotten Son, that whosoever believeth in him should not perish, but have everlasting life. — John 3:16 (KJV)

"I believe in the Holy Ghost, the holy catholic church, the communion of saints, the forgiveness of sins, the resurrection of the body, and the life everlasting. Amen!"

Life everlasting — the vast majority of folks do believe, some four out of five. Several years ago, the CBS magazine show *48 Hours*, devoted an entire program to life after death. It reported not only that more than 80% of Americans believe in an afterlife but also that two-thirds of all atheists believe as well. A *US News & World Report* cover story (3/31/97) asked, "Is there life after death?" The article stated, "As sophisticated medical technology has permitted more and more people to journey back from the brink of death, such seemingly mystical reports have become almost commonplace ... vivid images of tunnels of light, peaceful meadows, and angelic figures clad in white ... No matter what the nature of the experience, it alters some lives ... Hardened criminals opt for a life of helping others, atheists embrace the existence of a deity...."

Hmm. "I believe in the life everlasting." Of course, there is vast divergence on what that life will be like. Popular books and movies offer opinions. ABC did a movie some years back called *To Gillian on Her 37th Birthday*,[1] the sad story of a fellow whose wife had been killed in a boating accident two years before and who, to the detriment of everything else in his life, is maintaining a relationship with her ghost ... or is it just a hallucination? The movie did not seem quite sure.

The Robin Williams film a few years ago, *What Dreams May Come*,[2] *is* sure. It started off with Robin meeting the woman of his dreams Hollywood-style when their boats gently collide on a picturesque lake. One look and both knew they had found their soul mate, and before the credits had finished they were blissfully married with a pair of perfect children. Joyous as they were at the outset, that is how miserable they become when, out of nowhere, in more ways than one, repeated tragedies hit them, culminating in Robin's death when his physician character tries to be a good Samaritan at an accident scene.

Great guy that he is, Robin goes directly to heaven, leaving his wife to grow progressively miserable back on earth, so miserable, it turns out, that she commits suicide. Unfortunately, our filmmakers must have grown up with a medieval theology because that act of desperation plops her smack in the middle of hell. Her loving husband cannot abide that result so he works his way through a kind of Dante's "Inferno" of poor, tormented souls on an eternal rescue mission. To make a long story short, all comes out well in the end with a joyous family reunion that includes the family dalmatian and finally culminates in a good Buddhist reincarnation where we presume this will all be repeated over and over until they get it right.

With the closing credits we are left with a question Robin asks of his spirit-guide, "Where is God in all this?" The response: "Oh, up there. Somewhere. Shouting down that he loves us. Wondering why we can't hear him."

The producers of the film said their effort was to be understood as "spiritual" rather than "religious," and if they meant by that wanting to offer a conglomeration of traditions without any emphasis on just one, they succeeded. The movie was a theological mish-mash, but it was one more reminder of our natural fascination with what lies beyond this life. Of all creatures, we human beings are uniquely capable of contemplating our own mortality — that is why we are so interested in what we will find on the other side of death, and that is why so many can say from one tradition or another, or even no tradition at all, "I believe in the life everlasting."

Life everlasting — we are brought back to that wonderful text printed at the beginning of this chapter: "For God so loved the world that he gave his only begotten Son that whosoever believeth in him should not perish but have *everlasting life*." That offers a wonderful answer to Robin Williams' question, "Where is God in all this?" Right in the midst of it, Robin, and from beginning to end.

The text tells us that the initiative lies with God. Good. That clears up a misconception. Christianity is sometimes presented like so: gruff old Father God in heaven, furious with humanity and ready to destroy every last specimen; but then loving Jesus came along who went so far in seeking our pardon that he offered his own life as a sacrifice on the cross. Humanity was saved. Whew! This wonderful verse says that it was with God that it all started. Instead of being this gruff and grumpy old ogre, we read, "God so loved the world that...." God's initiative. As we noted in our last chapter, the Christian understanding of immortality ... *life everlasting* ... is that it is not a trait inherent to the human soul (Plato said that, not the Bible) — rather, it is a gift that is offered by a loving God.

Speaking of love, our verse says that is what motivates God. It is easy to think of God as looking at us in our heedlessness, our disobedience, our rebellion, and saying: "I will break them, I will discipline them, I will punish them until they straighten up." It is easy to think of God as seeking our allegiance in order to satisfy some divine desire for uncontested power. But not according to John 3:16 — God offers eternity out of simple love.

To whom? The whole world. Not one special nation, not just the good people — the world. The unlovable and the unlovely, the lonely who have no one else to love them, the one who loves God and the one who never thinks of God, the one who rests in the love of God and the one who spurns it — all are included in this vast inclusive love of God. As Augustine had it: "God loves each one of us as if there was only one of us to love." The *world*.

How do we take advantage of this divine initiative? Simple faith. "Whosoever believeth...." No great act of devotion, no special sacrifice, no merit on our own at all, in fact: "For it is by grace you have been saved, through faith — and this not from yourselves, it is the gift of God — not by works, so that no one can boast" (Ephesians 2:8-9) — *whosoever*.

The final outcome? "... shall not perish but have everlasting life." A life without the tyranny of time. As one commentator has it:

Here below, time withers flowers and human beauty, it encourages good intentions to evaporate, it deprives us of our loved ones. Within the universe ruled by time, the happiest marriage ends in death, the loveliest woman becomes a skeleton. Fading and aging, losing and failing, being deprived and being frustrated — these are the negative aspects of life in time. Life in eternity will liberate us from all loss, all deprivation.[3]

Yes! "I believe in the life everlasting." Tell me more. Details, details. What will it be like? The Bible is rather closed-mouth on the subject until we come to the book of Revelation, and that, my friend, as we have said before, is better understood as poetic, not photographic. We find the throne of God fronted by a sea of crystal and framed by a rainbow, thunder and lightning everywhere, attended by 24 elders dressed in white and praised eternally by four strange-looking winged beasts; "Day and night without ceasing they sing, 'Holy, holy, holy, the Lord God the almighty, who was and is and is to come' " (4:2-8 NRSV). A little scary at first blush. But then there are promises — God's final victory over oppressive systems, the end of evil and sin, and finally, "He will wipe every tear from their eyes. Death will be no more; mourning and crying and pain will be no more ..." (21:4 NRSV). Glory!

"I believe in the life everlasting." No, the Bible does not say a great deal about the life to come. As we noted in our preceding chapter, perhaps the reason is that we would not understand if it did — we have not reached the level of maturity that would allow us to comprehend. Nothing in our experience would help us to form the appropriate picture. As Paul says, "no eye has seen, nor ear heard, nor the human heart conceived, what God has prepared for those who love him" (1 Corinthians 2:9 NRSV).

Another reason may be equally important. God does not want us to have our eyes so firmly fixed on heaven that we are no earthly good. We have work to do right here. Over and over again in the scriptures, attention is turned away from speculations on future possibilities to imperatives concerning the present. By faith we say *this* is what I am called to do now; what comes after rests with God, the same God who is said to have "so loved the world that he gave his only begotten son that whosoever believeth in him should not perish but have everlasting life."

Yes, we continue to insist that as we believe, so we behave. When we know that this life is only the prelude to another, and that the other is infinitely superior to this one, it has a positive effect on everything we think or do. Our priorities change. Money, power, fame, the values of this world lose their luster in the light of the *next*. Instead, we learn to live now with a better and more satisfying perspective.

"I believe in the life everlasting." Something wonderful is on the way. David Redding, in his book, *God is Up to Something*, says, "Anyone who feels sorry for a dead Christian, as though the poor chap were missing something, is himself missing the transfiguring promotion involved. This is what we mean by the good news."[4]

There is a wonderful old story of a woman who had been diagnosed with cancer and had been given three months to live. Her doctor told her to start making preparations to die (something we all should be doing all of the time). So she contacted her pastor and had him come to her house to discuss certain aspects of her final wishes. She told him which songs she wanted sung at the service, what scriptures she would like read, and what she wanted to be wearing. The woman also told her pastor that she wanted to be buried with her favorite Bible.

Everything was in order and the pastor was preparing to leave when the woman suddenly remembered something very important to her. "There is one more thing," she said excitedly.

"What's that?" came the pastor's reply.

"This is very important. I want to be buried with a fork in my right hand." The pastor stood looking at the woman not knowing quite what to say. "That shocks you, doesn't it?" the woman asked.

"Well, to be honest, I am puzzled by the request," said the pastor.

The woman explained. "In all my years of attending church socials and functions where food was involved (and honestly, food is an important part of any church event; spiritual or otherwise) my favorite part was when, whoever was clearing away the dishes of the main course would lean over and say, 'You can keep your fork.' It was my favorite part because I knew that something better was coming. When they told me to keep my fork I knew that something great was about to be given to me. It wasn't Jell-O™ or pudding. It was cake or pie — something with substance. So I just want people to see me there in that casket with a fork in my hand and I want them to wonder, 'What's with the fork?' Then I want you to tell them, 'Something better is coming, so keep your fork, too.' "

The pastor's eyes welled up with tears as he hugged the woman good-bye. He knew this would be one of the last times he would see her before her death. He also knew that that woman had a wonderful grasp of heaven and life everlasting. She *knew* that something better was coming.

At the funeral, people were walking by the woman's casket and they saw the pretty dress she was wearing and her favorite Bible and the fork placed in her right hand. Over and over the pastor heard the question, "What's with the fork?" And over and over he smiled.

During his message the pastor told the people of the conversation he had with the woman shortly before she died. He also told them about the fork and about what it symbolized to her. He told them how he could not stop thinking about the fork and said that they probably would not be able to stop thinking about it either. He was right. So the next time you reach down for your fork, let it remind you, oh so gently, that there is something better coming.

Yes, "I believe in the life everlasting." And, if you don't mind, I will keep my fork.

---

1. *To Gillian on Her 37th Birthday*, directed by Michael Pressman, written by David E. Kelley, based on the play by Michael Brady, produced by Marykay Powell and David E. Kelley, released by Triumph, 1996.

2. *What Dreams May Come*, directed by Vincent Ward, written by Ron Bass, based on a book by Richard Matheson, produced by Barnet Bain, released by Polygram Filmed Entertainment, 1998.

3. Harry Blamires, "The Eternal Weight of Glory," *Christianity Today*, 5/27/91, p. 30.

4. David A. Redding, *God is Up to Something* (Waco, Texas: Word, Inc., 1972), p. 107.

Questions For Reflection

1. For many, "life everlasting" has been presented as one long church service, but lots of folks would equate that with hell rather than heaven. What do you think?

2. How do you hope to spend your time in eternity?

3. What opportunities for personal growth would you hope that God has in store for us?

4. Billy Graham was once asked if there would be golf in heaven, and he responded, "If that's what it takes to make you happy, then there will be golf in heaven." What do you think?

5. What about our beloved pets? Scripture says nothing about them. What do you think?